# The Centenary Match
# Kasparov-Karpov III

## RAYMOND KEENE

## DAVID GOODMAN

COLLIER BOOKS
Macmillan Publishing Company
New York

Macmillan Publishing Company
866 Third Avenue, New York, N.Y. 10022
Collier Macmillan Canada, Inc.


ISBN 0-02-028700-3


Macmillan books are available at special discounts for bulk purchases for sales promotions, premiums, fund-raising, or educational use. For details, contact:

>Special Sales Director
>Macmillan Publishing Company
>866 Third Avenue
>New York, N.Y. 10022

10 9 8 7 6 5 4 3 2 1

Printed in the United Kingdom

# Contents

# Acknowledgments

Our thanks to Dr Jacqueline Levy for editing and typing, especially the introductory material; Annette Keene for typing and constant encouragement; Phil Walden and IM Jon Tisdall of Reuters for valuable suggestions and help with proofs; Andek for their usual speedy typesetting; IM Bob Wade for references; Angela Day for typing; Pamela Divinsky for secretarial help; Simon Brougham for move times; GM Eddie Gufeld for analysis, especially for game 13; GM Dr Nikolai Krogius of the USSR Chess Federation for hospitality; Vladimir Kulyashov of the USSR Sports Committee for his friendly help in Leningrad; Paul Lamford and Graham Hillyard for proofreading and analytical suggestions, especially for game 18; IM elect Malcolm Pein for opening notes to game 19; Alex and Bobby Cox, Stewart Reuben and David Last for couriering material from Leningrad to London and back; all the telex staff at the Hotel Leningrad; Andy Rosenthal and the staff of AP Moscow, Edie Lederer and Larry Thorson of AP London, journalists Frank Guiral and Leontxo Garcia for background information; the *Times*, *Spectator*, *Leningradskaya Pravda*, *Chess Life*, the *M.I.Chigorin Special Bulletin* and *Sovietsky Sport* for permission to quote material; GM elect Max Dlugy for use of his notes from the London match bulletin; Richard Sams for writing up telexes and preparing diagrams; and all the purchasers of our last book who helped it sell out within eight days!

Raymond Keene
David Goodman
Leningrad, October 1986

*One town's very like another, when your head's down over your pieces, brother.* (Tim Rice, "One Night In Bangkok" from *Chess*)

# 1 The History of the World Championship

## BEFORE STEINITZ

Before the official title of World Champion was inaugurated in 1886 there were a number of players who could justly claim to be the strongest in the world, although there was not yet a formal championship.

The encounters between the Frenchman La Bourdonnais and McDonnell, who was Irish, were too diffuse to be seen as a real prototype for the modern title matches. These early contests were in fact a collection of small matches, although in the course of 1834 the two played no fewer than 88 games. The eventual score was 44 wins to La Bourdonnais and 30 to McDonnell, with 14 draws. Their play was notable for energy and ferocity rather than finesse.

The first match which closely resembled a modern world championship was the Staunton-St. Amant contest in Paris in 1843, which established an Englishman, Howard Staunton, as the foremost player in the world. Twenty-one games were played and Staunton scored eleven wins to his opponent's six:

*Paris 1843*

| | | | | | | | | | | | | | | | | | | | | | | |
|---|---|---|---|---|---|---|---|---|---|---|---|---|---|---|---|---|---|---|---|---|---|---|
| Staunton | 1 | 1 | ½ | 1 | 1 | 1 | 1 | 1 | 0 | 1 | 0 | 1 | 0 | ½ | 1 | 0 | ½ | ½ | 0 | 0 | 1 | **13** |
| St. Amant | 0 | 0 | ½ | 0 | 0 | 0 | 0 | 0 | 1 | 0 | 1 | 0 | 1 | ½ | 0 | 1 | ½ | ½ | 1 | 1 | 0 | **8** |

In 1851 the innovative and indefatigable Staunton organised the first ever international tournament, which was staged in London to coincide with the Great Exhibition held in Hyde Park that year. Participants included Staunton, Wyvill and Williams, but the German player Adolf Anderssen was the clear winner.

Seven years later when Paul Morphy, the undisputed American champion, arrived in Europe, he sought matches against the leading continental players and roundly beat Anderssen in a match played in Paris:

*Paris 1858*

| Morphy | 0 ½ 1 1 1 1 1 ½ 1 0 1 | **8** |
| Anderssen | 1 ½ 0 0 0 0 0 ½ 0 1 0 | **3** |

Anderssen lost another match in 1866 to Steinitz, who was fast establishing himself as the strongest of the Europeans:

*London 1866*

| Steinitz | 0 1 1 1 1 0 0 0 0 1 1 0 1 1 | **8** |
| Anderssen | 1 0 0 0 0 1 1 1 1 0 0 1 0 0 | **6** |

There have been claims that Steinitz's tenure of the World Championship truly dates back to this match, but it would have been undiplomatic, to say the least, to claim to be "World Champion" while Morphy still lived. Morphy died in 1884, having spent the last two decades of his life immersed in depression.

## ONE HUNDRED YEARS OF WORLD CHAMPIONSHIPS

The first official World Championship Match was played between Steinitz, an Austrian, and Zukertort, a Prussian, in 1886. Despite their continental origins, both men lived in England and London was the acknowledged chess capital of the world. The games in the 1886 match were played in three different cities – New York, St. Louis and New Orleans – thus setting a precedent for the peripatetic world championship, which was to repeated in 1894, 1908, 1910, 1929, 1934, 1935, 1937, 1948 and of course in 1986, with the current match split between London and Leningrad.

At first, however, World Champions picked their own opponents when they pleased, but financial pressures, public opinion and personal ambitions combined to produce fairly frequent title defences. The World Chess Federation did not come into being until 1924, and initially had little influence over the contests for the world championship.

The death of the reigning World Champion Alekhine in 1946 gave FIDE the chance to regularise the world title system. A democratic series of world-wide qualifying events was initiated, ensuring a fair chance for all. Matches were restricted to the best of 24 games, with an even score sufficient to maintain the status quo. The Champion was obliged to

2

defend at three-year periods, but had the right to a return match if he lost. The return match was abolished in 1963, but was reinstated by FIDE in 1978.

Another change was instituted for the 1978 match: the winner was to be the first to take six games. This was a modification of one of the demands made by World Champion Bobby Fischer, but he had already been deprived of his world title in 1975, when he refused to play Karpov. This may seem a trifle harsh when one takes into consideration the ten-year gap between Lasker's matches against Steinitz and Marshall, or Capablanca's six-year wait before defending his title against Alekhine. We are, however, now living in times when the absence of a contest at the top for more than three years is seen as a disaster for the development of world chess. In fact, though there was no world championship match between 1972 and 1978, there have now been no less than three between 1984 and 1986, and there is another due in 1987!

In 1984 the six-game rule led to the longest title match in the history of the championship. Although a marathon 48 games were played, the match was ended prematurely when the score stood at Karpov 5, Kasparov 3, with no less than 40 draws. The controversial decision to terminate the match was taken by FIDE President Florencio Campomanes, who explained that the match had "exhausted the physical, if not the psychological, resources not only of the participants, but of all those connected with the match." Just after Kasparov had won two games, the 47th and 48th, Campomanes declared the match to be indecisive and ruled that a new match would start in September 1985.

The re-match saw a return to the old rules with the number of games limited to 24. Kasparov emerged victorious when he won the 24th game to end the match with thirteen points to Karpov's eleven. Karpov then exercised his right to the revenge match, which is covered in this book.

## THE FIRST WORLD CHAMPIONSHIP MATCH

During the 1880s Wilhelm Steinitz and Johannes Zukertort had emerged as clearly superior to all of their contemporaries. Both of them claimed to be the strongest player in the world. After a series of bitter verbal exchanges the two men finally met at the chessboard to resolve their conflict.

Steinitz scored a decisive victory with ten wins to Zukertort's five. The new champion held the title until 1894, when he lost a match to Lasker.

A second defeat at Lasker's hands in 1896 was, perhaps, a partial cause of Steinitz's suffering a nervous breakdown, from which he never fully recovered. He died in a state of poverty as a public ward of the City of New York in 1900.

Steinitz was the chief promoter of the "Modern" school of chess, a system which rejected the pyrotechnics of sacrifices and combinations, concentrating instead on positional play aimed at the accumulation of small advantages.

The following two games, taken from the inaugural World Championship Match in 1886, show Steinitz in action.

### Zukertort-Steinitz
### Match (7) 1886
*Queen's Gambit Declined*

| | | |
|---|---|---|
| 1 | d4 | d5 |
| 2 | c4 | e6 |
| 3 | ♘c3 | ♘f6 |
| 4 | e3 | |

The modern choice here would most likely be 4 cd ed 5 ♗g5.

| | | |
|---|---|---|
| 4 | ... | c5 |
| 5 | ♘f3 | ♘c6 |
| 6 | a3 | dc |
| 7 | ♗xc4 | cd |
| 8 | ed | ♗e7 |
| 9 | 0-0 | 0-0 |
| 10 | ♗e3 | |

10 ♗g5 is more to the point.

| | | |
|---|---|---|
| 10 | ... | ♗d7 |
| 11 | ♕d3 | ♖c8 |
| 12 | ♖ac1 | ♕a5 |
| 13 | ♗a2 | ♖fd8 |
| 14 | ♖fe1 | |

Here 14 ♖fd1 looks stronger.

| | | |
|---|---|---|
| 14 | ... | ♗e8 |
| 15 | ♗b1 | g6 |
| 16 | ♕e2 | ♗f8 |
| 17 | ♖ed1 | ♗g7 |
| 18 | ♗a2 | ♘e7 |
| 19 | ♕d2 | ♕a6 |

White has been vacillating with no clear strategy in view. Meanwhile, Steinitz has been piling up pressure against White's d-pawn.

| | | |
|---|---|---|
| 20 | ♗g5 | ♘f5 |
| 21 | g4? | |

A desperate move, which should have been rejected in favour of 21 ♕c4.

| | | |
|---|---|---|
| 21 | ... | ♘xd4 |

A combination which throws a harsh searchlight on the weaknesses in White's camp. Indeed, even 21 ... ♘xg4 22 ♗xd8 ♖xd8

4

gives Black tremendous compensation for his modest investment.

| 22 | ♘xd4 | e5 |
| 23 | ♘d5 | ♖xc1 |
| 24 | ♕xc1 | ed |
| 25 | ♖xd4 | ♘xd5 |
| 26 | ♖xd5 | ♖xd5 |
| 27 | ♗xd5 | ♕e2 |
| 28 | h3 | h6 |
| 29 | ♗c4 | |

If 29 ♗xh6 ♗xh6 30 ♕xh6 ♕d1+.

| 29 | ... | ♕f3 |
| 30 | ♕e3 | ♕d1+ |
| 31 | ♔h2 | ♗c6 |
| 32 | ♗e7 | ♗e5+ |

A neat concluding combination to exploit the shattered nature of White's king's wing.

| 33 | f4 | |

Or 33 ♕xe5 ♕h1+ 34 ♔g3 ♕g2+ 35 ♔h4 ♕xf2+ 36 ♕g3 g5+ much as in the game.

| 33 | ... | ♗xf4+ |
| 34 | ♕xf4 | ♕h1+ |
| 35 | ♔g3 | ♕g1+ |

The finish would be 36 ♔h4 ♕e1+ 37 ♕g3 g5+ etc.

**0-1**

**Steinitz-Zukertort**
**Final (20th) Game, Match 1886**
*Vienna Gambit (Steinitz Variation)*

| 1 | e4 | e5 |
| 2 | ♘c3 | ♘c6 |
| 3 | f4 | |

This opening would never appear in a modern world championship match. The move 3 f4 gambits a key pawn from the kingside and is now considered far too weakening. Any player trying it now would be regarded as completely irresponsible.

| 3 | ... | ef |
| 4 | d4 | d5? |

This is now known to be incorrect. 4 ... ♕h4+ 5 ♔e2 d6! 6 ♘f3 ♗g4 firmly refutes White's play.

| 5 | ed | ♕h4+ |
| 6 | ♔e2 | ♕e7+ |
| 7 | ♔f2 | ♕h4+ |
| 8 | g3! | |

This bold move avoids a draw by repetition and Black's queen is now even more exposed than White's king.

| 8 | ... | fg+ |
|---|---|---|
| 9 | ♔g2 | ♘xd4 |
| 10 | hg | ♕g4 |
| 11 | ♕e1+ | ♗e7 |
| 12 | ♗d3 | ♘f5 |
| 13 | ♘f3 | ♗d7 |
| 14 | ♗f4 | f6 |
| 15 | ♘e4 | ♘gh6 |

This is a blunder by Black which allows a drastic termination.

| 16 | ♗xh6 | ♘xh6 |
|---|---|---|
| 17 | ♖xh6! | gh |
| 18 | ♘xf6+ | |

Exploiting the pin on the e-file to fork Black's king and queen.

| 18 | ... | ♔f8 |
|---|---|---|

Zukertort **resigned** before his queen was taken, thus making Steinitz the first official World Chess Champion.

Steinitz's gambit play in this game was, of course, atypical!

## The First World Championship Match
*New York, St Louis and New Orleans, 11 January-29 March 1886*

Steinitz   1 0 0 0 0 1 1 ½ 1 ½ 1 1 0 ½ ½ 1 ½ 1 1 1  **12½**

Zukertort 0 1 1 1 1 0 0 ½ 0 ½ 0 0 1 ½ ½ 0 ½ 0 0 0   **7½**

## THE WORLD CHAMPIONS 1886-1986

| | |
|---|---|
| **W.Steinitz**-I.Zukertort (USA 1886) | +10 – 5 = 5 |
| **W.Steinitz**-M.Chigorin (Havana 1889) | +10 – 6 = 1 |
| **W.Steinitz**-I.Gunsberg (New York 1890-91) | + 6 – 4 = 9 |
| **W.Steinitz**-M.Chigorin (Havana 1892) | +10 – 8 = 5 |
| W.Steinitz-**Em.Lasker** (USA/Canada 1894) | + 5 –10 = 4 |
| **Em.Lasker**-W.Steinitz (Moscow 1896-97) | +10 – 2 = 5 |
| **Em.Lasker**-F.Marshall (USA 1907) | + 8 – 0 = 7 |
| **Em.Lasker**-S.Tarrasch (Düsseldorf/Munich 1908) | + 8 – 3 = 5 |
| **Em.Lasker**-D.Janowski (Paris 1909) | + 7 – 1 = 2 |
| **Em.Lasker**-K.Schlechter (Vienna/Berlin 1910) | + 1 – 1 = 8 |
| **Em.Lasker**-D.Janowski (Berlin 1910) | + 8 – 0 = 3 |
| Em.Lasker-**J.R.Capablanca** (Havana 1921) | + 0 – 4 =10 |
| J.R.Capablanca-**A.Alekhine** (Buenos Aires 1927) | + 3 – 6 =25 |
| **A.Alekhine**-E.Bogoljubow (Germany/Holland 1929) | +11 – 5 = 9 |

**A.Alekhine**-E.Bogoljubow (Germany 1934)          + 8 – 3 =15
A.Alekhine-**M.Euwe** (Holland 1935)          + 8 – 9 =13
M.Euwe-**A.Alekhine** (Holland 1937)          + 4 –10 =11
**M.Botvinnik**
(The Hague/Moscow Match Tournament 1948)          +10 – 2 = 8
**M.Botvinnik**-D.Bronstein (Moscow 1951)          + 5 – 5 =14
**M.Botvinnik**-V.Smyslov (Moscow 1954)          + 7 – 7 =10
M.Botvinnik-**V.Smyslov** (Moscow 1957)          + 3 – 6 =13
V.Smyslov-**M.Botvinnik** (Moscow 1958)          + 5 – 7 =11
**M.Botvinnik**-M.Tal (Moscow 1960)          + 2 – 6 =13
M.Tal-**M.Botvinnik** (Moscow 1961)          + 5 –10 = 6
**M.Botvinnik**-T.Petrosian (Moscow 1963)          + 2 – 5 =15
**T.Petrosian**-B.Spassky (Moscow 1966)          + 4 – 3 =17
T.Petrosian-**B.Spassky** (Moscow 1969)          + 4 – 6 =13
B.Spassky-**R.Fischer** (Reykjavik 1972)          + 3 – 7 =11
**A.Karpov** (*by default* 1975)
**A.Karpov**-V.Korchnoi (Baguio City 1978)          + 6 – 5 =21
**A.Karpov**-V.Korchnoi (Merano 1981)          + 6 – 2 =10
A.Karpov-G.Kasparov (Moscow 1984-85)          + 5 – 3 =40
A.Karpov-**G.Kasparov** (Moscow 1985)          + 3 – 5 =16

# 2 The World Championship in London

## LONDON – CHESS CAPITAL OF THE WORLD

Foreign grandmasters are now commonly and gratifyingly talking of London as the world's chess capital, and for this we have to thank a number of sponsors, including Save and Prosper, the London Docklands Development Corporation, Lloyds Bank and, above all, the former Greater London Council.

The tradition of chess in London is vast. Can any other city boast chess played by all of the following illustrious names: Philidor, McDonnell, La Bourdonnais, Staunton, St Amant, Anderssen, Morphy, Zukertort, Nimzowitsch, Rubinstein, Réti and, of course, every world champion since the title was inaugurated in 1886? And every challenger too!

Only Moscow, with its immense sequence of world championship matches, can claim to better London's overall record.

In the foyer of Simpson's-in-the-Strand you can still see a chessboard and pieces of antique design on which all of the great 19th century champions displayed their skills.

London has naturally been the focus of some truly brilliant chess. Many of the game's unforgettable gems were produced here, including the Immortal Game, which was played at Simpson's:

**Anderssen-Kieseritzky**
**London 1851**
*King's Gambit*

| | | | | | |
|---|---|---|---|---|---|
| 1 | e4 | e5 | 8 | ♘h4 | ♕g5 |
| 2 | f4 | ef | 9 | ♘f5 | c6 |
| 3 | ♗c4 | ♕h4+ | 10 | ♖g1 | cb |
| 4 | ♔f1 | b5 | 11 | g4 | ♘f6 |
| 5 | ♗xb5 | ♘f6 | 12 | h4 | ♕g6 |
| 6 | ♘f3 | ♕h6 | 13 | h5 | ♕g5 |
| 7 | d3 | ♘h5 | 14 | ♕f3 | ♘g8 |
| | | | 15 | ♗xf4 | ♕f6 |
| | | | 16 | ♘c3 | ♗c5 |
| | | | 17 | ♘d5 | ♕xb2 |

| 18 | ♗d6 | ♛xa1+ | 21 | ♘xg7+ | ♔d8 |
|----|------|--------|----|-------|------|
| 19 | ♔e2 | ♗xg1 | 22 | ♕f6+ | ♘xf6 |
| 20 | e5 | ♘a6 | 23 | ♗e7 mate | |

In 1834 the La Bourdonnais-McDonnell series had been played in London, as were the games of the 1851 tournament, which was organised as a knockout competition.

In 1862 there was another powerful London tournament won by Anderssen ahead of Paulsen, while the 1866 Steinitz-Anderssen match was also played in London, as was the 1872 Steinitz-Zukertort match.

The London tournament of 1883 was the trigger for the 1886 world championship match, since it established the supremacy of Steinitz and Zukertort. The event was won by Zukertort with 22/26, followed by Steinitz in second place with 19.

This tournament proved to be an enormous undertaking – a 14-player double round-robin (all-play-all), where drawn games were initially discounted and then replayed to try and achieve a decisive result. This meant that the peaceably inclined Englisch and Rosenthal both had to play 45 games to reach their respective scores of 15½ and 14. Even the banquet was on a heroic scale and would have defeated many a modern grandmaster! Judge from the menu:

*Hors-d'-oeuvres.*
*Potages.*
Consommé aux Laitues Farcies.
Crême d'Asperges.

*Poissons.*
Saumon, Sauces Génévoise et Hollandaise.
Côtelettes de Homard, Sauce Riche.

*Entrées.*
Ris de Veau à la Printanière.
Noisettes de Mouton à la Chasseur.
Pommes Nouvelles.

*Relevé.*
Filet Piqué à la Portugaise.

*Rôtis.*
Poulet de Grains. Caneton.
Pommes Paille. Salade Française.

*Légume.*
Asperges, Sauce au Beurre.

*Entremets.*
Pêches Farcies aux Macarons.
Gelée aux Fraises. Petits Fours.
Ice Pudding.
Dessert.                           Coffee.

Over the next fifty years great tournaments continued to flourish: London 1899 (leading scores Lasker 23½/28, Janowski, Pillsbury, Maroczy 19); London 1922 (Capablanca, Alekhine, Vidmar, Rubinstein, Bogoljubow); the Olympiad (World Team Championship) of 1927 and then the same year the strong individual tournament won jointly by Tartakower and Nimzowitsch. Five years later the mighty World Champion Alekhine himself won first prize in what was to be the last of the great London events for many years (Alekhine, Flohr, Kashdan, Sultan Khan).

A final efflorescence came in the two-section tournament of 1946 (co-victors Steiner and Euwe) but then London had to wait until 1973 for its next grandmaster tournament, won by Jan Timman ahead of co-author Ray Keene, Hecht and Reshevsky.

In the 1980s the floodgates truly opened and we are now on our way to the restoration of London's 19th century supremacy. There have been the great GLC/Phillips & Drew tournaments of 1980, 1982, 1984 and the GLC solo effort of 1986; the world semi-finals of 1983 – Ribli v Smyslov and Kasparov v Korchnoi; the USSR-World match of 1984; the Commonwealth Championships of 1985 and 1986; and, of course, the Centenary World Championship itself.

## HOW LONDON GOT THE MATCH

In 1984 the British Chess Federation gave Ray Keene the task of bringing the world championship to England. As Chairman of the Match Organisation Committee, he immediately embarked on sounding out potential sponsors, but the BCF's first bid to hold a world title match was to fail and the 1985 match went to Moscow. Late in 1985 came a second chance, which finally brought the 1986 centenary world championship to London.

During the last few weeks of 1985 and the start of 1986 the British Chess Federation trod a frighteningly narrow path in its efforts to ensure firstly that Gary Kasparov did not default the return world championship match and secondly that all or part of the match be played in London.

Ultimately, the patient diplomacy of the BCF and its repeated willingness to accommodate the wishes of the players helped to avoid a potential tragedy, which might have been every bit as damaging to the chess world as Fischer's refusal to play for the world title in 1975.

Ironically, the current crisis had emanated from the surprise termination of the 1984/85 world championship by FIDE President Florencio Campomanes. That match was stopped "without decision", which effectively meant that the then World Champion, Anatoly Karpov, retained his title. Campomanes further declared that a new match was to start for the championship within six months.

Under new regulations this fresh contest was to be limited to 24 games. If the World Champion lost he was entitled to a further return match, which would prolong the 1982 championship cycle well into 1986. This was in fact to be the case.

But before that was to happen the 1985 encounter had to be staged, and the British Chess Federation hoped for the first time ever to put in a bid to hold a world championship match. The initial problem was to find adequate sponsorship.

The cost of such events had spiralled dramatically since the 1970s, when Fischer had single-handedly dragged chess out of its financial backwater. The famed Fischer-Spassky encounter of 1972 had attracted a prize fund of £100,000, half of it provided by British financier Jim Slater. By 1981 the prize fund had doubled to £200,000, and during the presidency of Campomanes it had been decreed that the minimum fund for a world match would be £300,000.

Backed by the Greater London Council and in particular by the far-sighted vision of Peter Pitt, chair of the GLC Arts and Recreation committees, the BCF was now able to put in a bid of one million Swiss francs for the rematch. The GLC had already sponsored a series of super-grandmaster tournaments in London between 1980 and 1986. Now the Council hoped to bring a match of the very highest calibre to the capital city. As Peter Pitt himself argued, the Council had a "strong commitment to investing in people's creativity, and what could be more creative than chess itself?".

Disappointingly, the BCF bid was topped by an offer of no less than 1,600,000 Swiss francs from Marseilles, surely sufficient to secure the match. But then Campomanes took the unprecedented step of asking the Russians to equal the biggest bid, which they did. Marseilles, the front runner, had been gazumped! As a condition of holding the match the Soviet Chess Federation was to concede 24% of the prize fund to CACDEC, the FIDE fund for developing countries, which is administered solely by the President.

11

Once again Moscow was to be the scene of a chess challenge between Karpov and Kasparov, and the match remained a cliff-hanger until the very end. In the 24th game Kasparov scored his vital fifth win, leaving him undisputed chess king of the world and the youngest world champion in the history of chess.

The euphoria of Kasparov and his ardent fans was soon tempered, however, by the knowledge that his reign as champion might also be the shortest on record. Karpov still had the right to another challenge and FIDE regulations stipulated that the third match in the series should start by 10 February 1986. Kasparov had the space of just three months to enjoy his new super-status.

Offers to hold the next stage in the cycle had to be assembled rapidly, and after further consultation with the GLC the British Chess Federation was able to make a bid of 1.8 million Swiss francs, or approximately £600,000. Peter Pitt wrote later that "when I led the GLC delegation to Lucerne . . . to make the bid to bring this world championship to London I was confident in both the size of the bid made and the capacity of London to host the match. All in all it has been very gratifying to see how effective this use of public money has been, as it will make London the focal point of world attention for the duration of the match. This initial input by the GLC has, I know, led to other quite considerable sponsorship from the private sector, but it must be remembered that without the initial move by the GLC none of this would have been possible."

The only other bid came from the Soviet federation, but would it be enough to leave British chess fans disappointed for a second time? On the appointed day, 16 December 1985, two sealed envelopes were opened at the FIDE headquarters in Lucerne. Leningrad was offering 1,000,000 Swiss francs. London's chances of hosting a world championship now appeared overwhelming. The British offer was nearly double the size of that from Russia. In addition, a new ruling prohibited any federation from holding two consecutive world matches.

Almost immediately, the British Chess Federation made it known that in the interests of détente it would be willing to split the match with twelve games in London and twelve in Leningrad. Now began the weeks of waiting for a final decision.

In reality, there were still a number of factors which could completely scupper London's hopes. The players had to consider their own preferences and the President of FIDE was to inspect the playing conditions personally to ensure that they were to standard. FIDE would not make the final announcement until 13 January 1986. Interwoven with these technical considerations was another formidable obstacle. Kasparov objected to being forced to defend his title so soon after the end of the last match. No previous champion had in fact ever defended his title in much less than a year.

On 23 December Kasparov gave a press conference in Amsterdam where he openly criticised FIDE's hasty timetabling for the new match and emphasised the fact that the right to a rematch had already been abolished for the future. He argued that "this match should not take place, because no one should have so many privileges. The World Champion keeps his title in a drawn match, and that should be enough. In future, I will not have a return match should I lose. According to the decision adopted by the FIDE Congress, I must be World Champion for at least a year – for 1986. I was told about the rematch to be given Karpov only a few days before the opening of the second match in Moscow. I had no time to protest against it."

In his opening statement Kasparov endorsed Professor Lincoln Lucena of Brazil running for the post of FIDE President on a joint reform ticket with co-author Keene: "In the past few years there have been a lot of problems in our chess world. During my stay here I have met with people who are prepared to work for more democracy in the world of chess. They want chessplayers to know what is going on. They want correct rules, and they want the wishes of the players to be respected. These are also my feelings. And as World Champion, I think it my duty to support the people working for these things. I wish Mr Lincoln Lucena and GM Ray Keene success in their campaign to reform FIDE.

"I am very happy to hear that the European Chess Union has been formed to look after the interests of the strongest chessplaying nations. The New Year is normally a time of peace, but you must fight sometimes to have that peace. I hope that in the next year we will return to genuine peace in chess and that chessplayers can then concentrate on creating beautiful games under normal conditions."

Rolf Littorin of Sweden, President of the newly formed European Chess Union, read the text of a message from the Union to the Soviet Chess Federation, asking that the rematch should not go ahead. Kasparov was supported by Dutch Grandmaster Jan Timman and messages in favour of his stand were received from absent grandmasters, including Bent Larsen of Denmark, Oscar Panno of Argentina and Lev Alburt of the USA.

The World Champion's objections to a rematch gave the BCF its biggest problem. As a national federation the BCF had a duty to attempt to bring the 1986 world title match to London. This was the centenary match and it would be the first time a world championship had been fought out on British soil. But the BCF also wished to ensure that both Karpov and Kasparov were satisfied with the conditions, which clearly extended to the scheduling of the match itself. An obvious compromise was to start the match later in 1986, in the summer or early autumn. This simple solution was fraught with dangers, for the main British sponsor, the GLC, was to be legally abolished on 1 April 1986. Could the offer of sponsorship continue past that crucial date?

Added to this dilemma was the question of whether Kasparov would participate at all. The World Champion's reluctance to play was not helped by the inflexible stand taken by the FIDE President. In an AP interview published on 31 December 1985 Campomanes threatened to strip Kasparov of the title on 7 January if he had not by then agreed to play.

In his haste Campomanes had misread his own rules, which only permit a champion to be defaulted if he fails to confirm that he will play two weeks after the venue is announced. A retraction of Campomanes's threat and a correction duly emerged from FIDE's Lucerne HQ on 7 January.

On 13 January, the deadline for an official FIDE announcement of the venue, Campomanes declared that no decision had yet been taken. The reason for the delay was a series of behind-the-scenes negotiations taking place between FIDE, the British Chess Federation, the Soviet Federation and the two competitors. On 20 January the BCF sent the following telex to its Soviet counterpart, stressing the need to ensure that Kasparov and Karpov were satisfied with any proposed settlement:

*Attention USSR Chess Federation*

*In answer to your telex of 86-01-16 concerning reintroduction of return match for the future world championship cycles: it is our view that the reinstatement of a return match would be inadvisable in a two year world championship cycle. Such a reintroduction would lead to congestion of*

14

*international tournament schedules. We stress, however, that it is ideally a matter which the players concerned should decide themselves.*

*We take this opportunity to repeat our offer that should the return world championship match of the current cycle go ahead then London, the BCF and the GLC are very willing to stage the first 12 games here with the second 12 in Leningrad. It is in our view essential though that any problems concerning the staging of the return match should be amicably settled to the mutual satisfaction of both World Champion Kasparov and Challenger Karpov. It is of extreme importance that no public problems damage the international chess movement and its reputation worldwide. In particular, we would wish to avoid the unseemly default situations which occurred in 1975 and 1983.*

*Regards*

*David Jarrett*
*President*

*David Anderton*
*International Director*

*Ray Keene*
*FIDE Delegate*

*British Chess Federation*

The players now took matters into their own hands. With the full backing of their own federation Kasparov and Karpov signed an agreement in Moscow on 22 January in order, in their own words, "to avoid a situation where, in the absence of an agreement, they would have to accept any extraordinary measures decided by FIDE". They agreed that a return match would take place, but it would be postponed until the summer. Here is the full text of their joint statement:

*World Champion Gary Kasparov and ex-World Champion Anatoly Karpov, having examined the complicated situation that was created during the world championship competition and wanting to eliminate differences of opinion and avoid a situation where, in the absence of an agreement, they would have to accept any extraordinary measures decided by FIDE, have agreed the following:*

15

*1) The return match between them as foreseen by 1985 FIDE rules will take place.*

*2) It is to begin in July or August 1986. This postponement from the date set up earlier is necessary for both chessplayers, in order to rest and restore their strength after having played 72 games against each other in 14 months.*

*3) Hoping that the wish will meet with the understanding of the leadership of FIDE and the whole chess world, they think a super final (the match between the winner of the Candidates and the ex-World Champion) will take place in February 1987 and the next world championship match in July or August 1987.*

*4) Kasparov and Karpov have undertaken the following obligations towards each other:*

*a) neither of them will play a match with the winner of the Candidates' cycle until the return match between them is over;*

*b) the winner of the return match guarantees the loser that he will not play a world championship match with the winner of the Candidates cycle until that player has played a match against the ex-World Champion;*

*c) under all circumstances our position as stated in a) and b) will stay permanent.*

*After examining the bids for the organisation of the return match from the cities of Leningrad and London received by the President of FIDE dated 16 December 1985, Kasparov and Karpov expressed their wish to play the match in Leningrad. If, however, the organisers of either of them withdraw their bids in connection with the changed dates of the match the participants are ready to consider other bids which are made in accordance with FIDE regulations by 1 April 1986 so that the venue, dates of return match and the team of arbiters can be announced a month later.*

*Signed in Moscow 22 January 1986*

*1* Gary Kasparov *2* Anatoly Karpov *3 Approved by the Executive Council of the Soviet Chess Federation unanimously* V.Sevastianov *(USSR Federation President)*

Faced with this *fait accompli* on the part of the two principals and their federation, FIDE had no option but to accept. A week later Campomanes released his own statement. The match was to start between 28 July and 4 August and would be split between London and Leningrad:

*1) The return match between World Champion Gary Kasparov and ex-World Champion Anatoly Karpov will start between 28 July and 4 August 1986. The exact date is to be fixed in consultation with the organisers.*
*2) Since the Graz FIDE Congress in 1985 decided that future world championship matches should be organised by other federations and whereas the players had expressed a wish to play in Leningrad, the match shall be played in two parts: 1st in London and 2nd in Leningrad.*
*3) FIDE considers that the match will be a better match if it is played entirely in one place, therefore the match could be played entirely in London after consultation with the British Chess Federation and the USSR Chess Federation.*

Although delighted that an acceptable solution had been found, BCF officials were now deeply worried that the GLC, with abolition looming, would no longer be able to provide sponsorship. On 1 April 1986 the Council would hand over responsibility to the London Residuary Body. Only then would this new institution decide whether the promised funding could go ahead.

Faced with such uncertainty the BCF, nevertheless, continued to plan for the match. Such an important event could not be thrown together hastily at the last minute and it would be better to cancel existing arrangements later on, rather than be trapped with insufficient time to stage the match properly. A World Championship Organisation Committee had already been formed, consisting of Peter Pitt, representing the GLC, and three BCF representatives: David Anderton, Match Adviser, Ray Keene, Chairman of the Committee, and Stewart Reuben. The latter was the BCF's Director of Congress Chess and had been responsible for organising the British Championship and the Lloyds Bank Masters tournaments in past years.

The Committtee eventually picked the Park Lane Hotel as the most suitable site for the match. During the Second World War the Grand Ballroom at the hotel had been chosen as an alternative venue for Parliament in the event of bombing at Westminster. Now the ballroom was to house the paraphernalia of a world championship. A stage would have to be erected, new overhead lighting installed for the players, and rooms built where Karpov and Kasparov could rest during the games.

While these decisions were being taken, the BCF watched anxiously as 1 April drew near. When the new London Residuary Body finally considered the case for funding the match their conclusion was noncommittal. It was now the responsibility of Westminster, the chosen site for the match. With weeks to go before the scheduled starting date, the BCF approached anyone who might be able to argue in favour of the match. Letters were despatched to Nigel Lawson, the Chancellor of the Exchequer, and Peter Brooke, the Treasury Minister. The help of chess enthusiast and MP for Richmond and Barnes, Jeremy Hanley, was enlisted. Chess-playing Westminster ratepayers even telephoned their local councillor late at night to put the case for bringing high-level chess to London.

Under such a bombardment Westminster Council acquiesced – the match was safe and the finalised plans could power ahead. In accordance with the regulations, Campomanes, Karpov and Kasparov all travelled separately to London for an inspection of the playing conditions. With some provisos, all three pronounced their satisfaction with the organisation.

On his visit Kasparov proved to be the most outspoken of the three, even appearing on the popular BBC chat programme *Wogan*, where he berated FIDE officials as members of the "international mafia" and praised Britain as being the only place free of "this mafia". In an interview with *Time Out* reporter Peter Willis, Kasparov warmed to this theme, explaining that he had to win the next title match "for the future of world chess. It's very important for me and for chess because now I'm sure, and my friends are sure too, that I am defending chess against an international chess mafia."

Kasparov's visit to London coincided with the opening of the new Tim Rice/Abba musical *Chess*, which is loosely based on the lives of Fischer, Korchnoi, Karpov and Kasparov. The musical proved immediately popular and on the opening night was booked up for months to come. It was becoming increasingly difficult for the British public to avoid the subject of chess.

In order to capitalise on the massive international publicity connected with the musical and the world title match, the BCF had already declared 1986 to be London Chess Year, and a great summer chess festival was planned with peripheral chess events all over the country. The Kleinwort Grieveson British Chess Championships were due to start at Southampton on 28 July, the same day that the Kasparov-Karpov match would start at the Park Lane Hotel. From 9-17 August events would take place at the Barbican and the Commonwealth Open Chess Championship would be held at the Great Eastern Hotel from 11-19 August, alongside the Lloyds Bank Junior and Masters tournaments. Further events were taking place in Manchester and Buckinghamshire, and the Welsh had chosen Swansea for the British Isles Open Tournament in September.

Television programmes were planned for the BBC and ITV throughout the duration of the match, offering grandmaster analysis of the games and visual coverage of the two protagonists at the board. The grand design was to saturate Britain with chess throughout the summer and to build on the fast-growing prominence and status of chess in Britain.

Stewart Reuben declared that it was the BCF's intention "that London . . . will be permeated with chess, such that people will talk of it when they walk the streets, sing of it in their bath, and most particularly teach it to their children."

# 3  Profile of Gary Kasparov

**Born 13.4.63**
**World Champion 1985-**
**Rating at 1.7.86: 2740**

Kasparov has always acknowledged two leading influences in his chess career: Alekhine and Botvinnik. The brilliant games of Alekhine inspired him, but Kasparov has also had the good fortune to have studied personally under Botvinnik in his famous training school. Indeed, it is one of Kasparov's ambitions to establish worldwide branches of the school, to be run by accredited trainers.

Kasparov's rise to World Champion has been astoundingly meteoric, although his immense talent was evident from the start. When he was only 11 Botvinnik wrote prophetically: "The future of chess lies in the hands of this young man".

Kasparov qualified as an International Grandmaster in 1980 at the age of 17, and two years later he was rated as the second strongest player in the world. In November 1985, aged 22, he became the youngest world champion in the history of the official championship. In recognition of his achievements Kasparov was honoured with the "chess oscar" in 1982, 1983 and 1985.

What secrets did Botvinnik impart to his young acolyte? One important technique which Kasparov has acquired is the art of deep research through training matches with his aides. Botvinnik kept his own efforts in this vein secret for many years, but eventually made them public in his autobiographical record of his best games.

Kasparov's last match in London was in 1983, when he defeated Viktor Korchnoi in the Candidates semi-final which set him on the path to the world championship. In 1984 he played second board in the exciting and fiercely contested USSR v Rest of the World match held in London Docklands, the Soviet side eventually taking victory by the narrow margin of 21-19.

During 1984 and 1985 Kasparov twice played Karpov for the world title, contesting a total of 72 games. Kasparov was to come to speak of Karpov as "my permanent opponent". Throughout the course of these difficult encounters Kasparov displayed an astonishing buoyancy and resilience of spirit.

## MATCH VERSUS TIMMAN

A little over a month after he won the world championship in 1985, Kasparov played a six-game challenge match in Hilversum against the then world number 3, Dutch grandmaster Jan Timman.

The match was of immense importance. It was the first time since the days of Lasker at the beginning of the century that a world chess champion had willingly agreed to contest a challenge with a leading rival, without first making that player go through complex financial or qualifying hoops.

In addition, the games played in Hilversum were outstanding, comprising some of the most combinative and exciting ever played at this level. When Timman resigned after the sixth game, conceding the match by the score of 4-2, hundreds of chess fans stormed the stage to catch a glimpse of their heroes analysing what might have been.

Here is Timman's only win from the match, which demonstrates that he too was in fine form. Kasparov just proved to be the stronger of the two in this extraordinary clash of titans.

**Timman-Kasparov, match (3) 1985.** *Ruy Lopez.*
**1 e4 e5 2 ♘f3 ♘c6 3 ♗b5 a6 4 ♗a4 ♘f6 5 0-0 ♗e7 6 ♖e1 b5 7 ♗b3 d6 8 c3 0-0 9 h3 ♗b7 10 d4 ♖e8 11 ♘g5 ♖f8 12 ♘f3 ♖e8 13 ♘bd2 ♗f8 14 a3 h6 15 ♗c2 ♘b8 16 b4 ♘bd7 17 ♗b2 g6 18 c4 ed 19 cb ab 20 ♘xd4 c6 21 a4 ba 22 ♗xa4 ♕b6 23 ♘c2 ♕c7 24 ♗b3 ♗a6 25 ♖c1 ♗g7 26 ♘e3 ♗b5 27 ♘d5 ♘xd5 28 ♗xg7 ♔xg7 29 ed ♘e5 30 ♘e4 ♘d3 31 ♕d2 ♖a3?.** Much too ambitious. **31 ... ♕e7!** is good for Black. **32 ♘f6!!.**

A staggering shot which utterly reverses the roles. Now White is on the attack. **32 ... ♖xe1+ 33 ♖xe1 ♔xf6 34 ♕c3+ ♘e5 35 f4 ♗a4? 36 fe+ de 37 d6 ♕xd6 38 ♕f3+ ♔e7 39 ♕xf7+ ♔d8 40 ♖d1 ♖a1 41 ♕f6+ 1-0**

The final game of the match featured a splendid knight sacrifice:

**Kasparov-Timman, match (6) 1985.** *Queen's Indian.*
**1 d4 ♘f6 2 c4 e6 3 ♘f3 b6 4 ♘c3 ♗b4 5 ♗g5 ♗b7 6 e3 h6 7 ♗h4 g5 8 ♗g3 ♘e4 9 ♕c2.** In game 2 of the match Kasparov had tried the gambit **9 ♘d2. 9 ... ♗xc3+ 10 bc d6 11 ♗d3 f5 12 d5 ♘c5 13 h4 g4 14 ♘d4 ♕f6 15 0-0 ♘xd3.** Hoping to improve on his play in game 4, where 15 ... ♘1a6 16 ♘xe6 ♘xe6 17 ♗xf5 granted White a vehement attack for the sacrificed piece. **16 ♕xd3 e5.** White's pressure against the black pawns on e6 and f5 forces Black to relinquish their cohesion. But Timman has a neat tactical point in mind. **17 ♘xf5 ♗c8 18 ♘d4!**

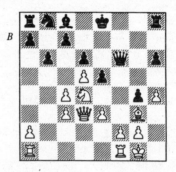

*B*

A splendid sacrifice of a piece, for which White gains a mobile mass of central pawns. Kasparov told co-author Keene that the idea came to him only five minutes before the game started. In contrast 18 e4 defending the knight is bad after 18 ... ♗xf5 19 ef ♘d7. **18 ... ed 19 cd ♕f5!**. An excellent defensive resource, which Kasparov had underestimated. The World Champion had only anticipated 19 ... ♘d7, when 20 f4! followed by e4 gives an overwhelming attack. Timman's method slows White down. **20 e4 ♕g6 21 ♕c3 0-0 22 ♖fe1 ♘d7 23 e5 ♗b7 24 ♖e3 b5?**. Having conducted an excellent defence, Timman goes astray with an apparently logical move to undermine White's queenside. Correct was 24 ... ♖ae8, rushing all his reserves to the centre. **25 ♕a5!**. Inaugurating a forcing sequence of moves whereby White either wins a large number of pawns or transfers his queen into the heart of the black king's defences. **25 ...**

♘b6 26 ♕xb5 ♕c2 27 ed cd 28 ♖e7 ♖f7 29 ♖xf7 ♔xf7 30 c5 ♕c4 31 ♕b1!. An original switch back. Black still has no choice. **31 ... ♕xd5 32 ♕h7+ ♔f6 33 ♕xh6+ ♔f7 34 ♕f4+ ♔g8 35 ♕xg4+ ♔h7 36 ♗f4!**. The final link in the chain. Apart from defending g2, the point is to parry 36 ... ♖g8 with 37 ♗g5 followed by ♕h5+. Kasparov had to see this move as far back as 28 ♖e7. **36 ... ♗c8 37 ♕g3 dc 38 ♖e1 ♕f7 39 ♕g5 ♘d5 40 ♕h6+ ♔g8 41 ♖e5 1-0**. If 41 ... ♕xf4 42 ♖e8+ or 41 ... ♘xf4 42 ♖g5+.

The final score in the match was as follows:

**Hilversum, December 1985**

| | | | | | | | |
|---|---|---|---|---|---|---|---|
| Kasparov | 1 | 1 | 0 | ½ | ½ | 1 | **4** |
| Timman | 0 | 0 | 1 | ½ | ½ | 0 | **2** |

## MATCH VERSUS MILES

In May 1986 Kasparov played another match in Basel against English GM Tony Miles, crushing him by the sort of score – 5½-½ – that only Fischer used to achieve. This was an indication that Kasparov was in increasingly formidable form – rather better, in fact, than Karpov was in at the SWIFT tournament held in Brussels earlier in 1986. According to Bob Wade their relative individual Elo rating performances were 3040 for Kasparov at Basel and 2811 for Karpov in Brussels.

The published figures for Kasparov and Karpov over the past five years are particularly interesting. Karpov twice reached a personal peak of 2725 before 1982, but from January 1982 until July 1986 he stayed firmly between 2700 and 2720. During that same period Kasparov shot up from 2640 to 2740 and may well be improving at a faster rate than Fischer did at the same age.

For the purposes of rough comparison, Fischer's rating had shot into the 2500s before he was 17; by 22 he had reached 2700, and at the age of 29 in 1972, when he had won the world championship, he had pushed his rating to 2780, the highest Elo ever recorded.

Here is the amazing sixth game from the Miles match:

**Miles-Kasparov, match (6) Basel, May 1986.** *Slav (Meran).*
**1 d4 d5 2 c4 c6 3 ♘c3 ♘f6 4 e3 e6 5 ♘f3 ♘bd7 6 ♗d3 dc 7 ♗xc4 b5 8 ♗d3 a6 9 e4 c5 10 e5 cd 11 ♘xb5 ♘g4 12 ♕a4**. With the score at 4½-½ against him, it must have taken real courage to play such a double-edged variation in the final game. Afterwards Miles agreed, saying "I knew I was probably crazy to play 12 ♕a4". **12 ... ♘gxe5 13 ♘xe5**

♘xe5 14 ♘d6+. In the *Encyclopaedia of Chess Openings* Korchnoi gives 14 ♘c7+ ♚e7 15 ♘xa8 ♖xd3+ 16 ♚e2 ♘e5 17 ♕b4+ ♚e8 18 ♕b6 ♕xb6 19 ♘xb6 leading to a big advantage in the endgame. But much better is 17 ... ♚f6! 18 ♕d2 ♚e7! with equality. **14 ... ♚e7 15 ♘xc8+ ♚f6!?.** For the second time in the match (as in game 3) Kasparov declines to recapture a knight that has taken a bishop. **16 ♗e4.** If 16 ♗xa6 ♘d3+ 17 ♚e2 ♘b4! (17 ... ♘c5 18 ♕c6 d3+ 19 ♚d1 ♕d5 20 ♕xd5 ed 21 ♘b6 is better for White) 18 ♕b5 h6 (or 18 ... ♚g6) 19 ♗b7 ♖a5 20 ♕c4 ♖c5 is unclear. But 17 ♚f1 ♘b4 or ♘c5 18 ♕d1! is stronger, intending ♕f3+. **16 ... ♖xc8 17 h4?.** 17 0-0 ♖c4! 18 ♕xa6 d3 is fine for Black, e.g. 19 f4 ♕d4+ 20 ♚h1 ♘g4. Nevertheless, 17 0-0 would have been the correct course. Miles had overlooked a tactical point, and in the further course of the game the weak point on h4 is of great use to Black. **17 ... h6 18 0-0.** Miles had missed a complex variation, namely that 18 ♗g5+ is answered by 18 ... hg 19 hg+ ♚xg5 20 ♖xh8 ♖c4! 21 ♕b3 ♗b4+ 22 ♕xb4 ♕xh8 23 ♕d2+ ♚f6 24 ♕f4+ ♚e7!, when Black is much better. **18 ... ♖c4 19 ♕d1 d3 20 ♖e1 ♖xc1! 21 ♖xc1 d2 22 ♖f1 ♕d4.**

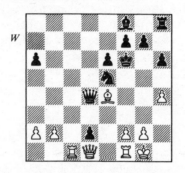

If now 23 ♖c8 ♕xe4 24 ♕xd2 ♗b4 25 ♕e3 ♘f3+!! and Black wins. **23 ♖c2 ♕xe4 24 ♖xd2 ♗c5 25 ♖e1 ♕xh4 26 ♕c2 ♗b4 27 ♖xe5.** If 27 ♖e4 ♘f3+! 28 gf ♕g5+ wins. **27 ... ♗xd2 28 g3 ♕d4 29 ♖e4 ♕d5 0-1.** These notes were dictated to co-author Keene by Kasparov in his suite at the Sarria Hotel on 3 June 1986, following his presentation earlier in the day with the "Chess Oscar" by *El Corte Ingles* for the best performance of 1985.

After this final game Miles was asked about Kasparov. "I thought I was playing the World Champion – not some 27-eyed monster who sees everything", he exclaimed.

# 4   Profile of Anatoly Karpov

**Born 23.5.51**
**World Champion 1975-1985**
**Rating at 1.7.86: 2705**

During his ten-year reign as world champion, Anatoly Karpov proved to be an active and successful representative for chess all over the world. He won more major tournaments than any previous world champion, including Skopje 1976, Montreal 1979 and London 1984.

His incumbency was in stark contrast to that of his immediate predecessor, Robert Fischer of the USA, who did not play a single game of chess in public after he won the world title in 1972. In 1975 Karpov won the world championship by default, since Fischer did not defend his title, but Karpov's results since then have been formidable, not only in tournaments but also in match play. He defeated Viktor Korchnoi in world championship matches in 1978 and 1981, the second time by a margin of 11-7. Between 1973 and 1984 he was awarded the "chess oscar" an unprecedented total of nine times. He will undoubtedly go down in history as one of the greatest of world champions.

## *BRUSSELS 1986*

After he lost the world title last year Karpov soon brushed aside any suspicion that he might be jaded or off form by winning two major tournaments, the SWIFT tournament in Brussels and the Bugojno tournament. In Brussels he dominated a field which included his old rival Korchnoi, plus such dangerous younger opponents as Timman, Ljubojević and Miles. Karpov's marathon 105-move win against Jan Timman and his dramatic demolition of the top Yugoslav Ljubojević were particularly impressive.

Karpov is best characterised as a student of the modern school of chess, building on small advantages in order to create winning positions. His style may be deemed quiet, but it is of awesome accuracy, as can be seen from the following superb win from the SWIFT tournament.

25

**Karpov-Ljubojević, Brussels 1986.** *French Defence.*
**1 e4 e6 2 d4 d5 3 ♘d2 ♘f6.** Karpov has a tremendous track record against this line of the Tarrasch Variation. Black's third move invites White to seize vast tracts of central terrain. Black then hopes to penetrate this extended structure. Karpov, however, is an adept at keeping the space advantage and parrying any counterplay. Korchnoi has been very successful at obtaining draws against Karpov with the more fluid 3 ... c5, but this inevitably leads to the need for patient defence, which does not suit everybody. **4 e5 ♘fd7 5 c3 c5 6 f4 ♘c6 7 ♘df3 ♕b6 8 g3 a5.** Black hopes to strike out with ... a4, but Karpov promptly squashes this possibility. **9 a4 cd 10 cd ♗b4+ 11 ♔f2.** White avoids exchanges now, because Black's forces are very cramped. **11 ... g5.** A wild attempt at counterplay, which may simply serve to undermine the solidity of his own position. **12 h3 f6 13 ♗e3 0-0 14 ♖c1 ♖f7 15 ♖h2.** An exemplary Karpov move. ♖h2 might look insignificant, but in fact it is very far-sighted. Later this rook's positioning on the second rank will play a decisive role. **15 ... ♗f8 16 ♕d2 ♕b4 17 ♕xb4 ab 18 b3 ♘a5 19 ♖b1 gf 20 gf ♗h6 21 ♗d3 b6 22 ♖g2+ ♔h8 23 ♘e2 ♗a6.** Logically seeking to obtain further relief by exchanges and at the same time dispense with the services of the queen's bishop, which is severely hemmed in. Karpov's refutation is both crushing and artistic. **24 ♗xa6 ♖xa6 25 f5!**

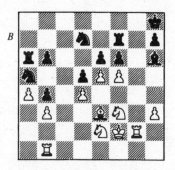

The decisive coup. White both gains material and launches a deadly attack on the black king. **25 ... ♗xe3+ 26 ♔xe3 b5.** If 26 ... ef 27 e6 ♖e7 28 ♘f4 with threats of ♖bg1 or ♘h4, while 26 ... fe 27 fe ed+ 28 ♔f2 leaves Black without enough compensation for the lost material. **27 ab ♖b6 28 ♖bg1.** Threatening mate on the back rank. **28 ... h5 29 ♘f4 fe 30 ♘g6+ ♔h7 31 ♘g5+ ♔g7 32 ♘xe5 ♘xe5 33 ♘xf7+ ♔xf7 34 de 1-0.**

## BUGOJNO 1986

From Brussels Karpov moved on to the small Yugoslavian town of Bugojno, where one of the strongest tournaments – perhaps *the* strongest – in the history of chess was staged in May and June 1986. The other players were Miles, Sokolov, Yusupov, Timman, Portisch, Ljubojević and Spassky. Karpov lost a game at the beginning to Sokolov, giving rise to unfounded rumours that he was out of form. This was in fact the first time a Soviet player had beaten Karpov in a tournament outside the USSR since he became world champion in 1975.

Here is the game:

**Sokolov-Karpov, Bugojno 1986.** *Ruy Lopez.*
**1 e4 e5 2 ♘f3 ♘c6 3 ♗b5 a6 4 ♗a4 ♘f6 5 0-0 ♗e7 6 ♖e1 b5 7 ♗b3 d6.** Karpov never plays the Marshall Gambit, so there was no point in bluffing with 7 ... 0-0. **8 c3 0-0 9 h3 ♗b7 10 d4 ♖e8 11 ♘g5.** A harmless excursion often played to gain time on the clock. **11 ... ♖f8 12 ♘f3 ♖e8 13 ♘bd2 ♗f8 14 ♗c2.** Alternatives here are 14 d5 ♘e7 15 ♗c2 g6 16 ♘f1 ♗g7 17 b3, when Black can try the interesting sacrifice 17 ... ♘xe4, as in Geller-Eingorn, Riga 1985, and 14 a4 ♕d7, as tried in Kasparov-Karpov, match (46) Moscow 1984/85. **14 ... ♘b8 15 a4 c5.** This may be suspect. White is encouraged to play d5, locking in his opponent's queen's bishop, when Black no longer has the possibility of undermining White's central bastions with ... c6. 15 ... ♘bd7 is preferable. **16 d5 ♘bd7 17 b4 c4 18 ♘f1 ♘h5 19 ♘3h2 g6.** 19 ... ♘f4 looks more active. **20 ♗e3 ♗e7 21 ♕d2 ♖f8 22 ♗h6 ♘g7 23 ♘g3 ♔h8.** The problem here is that the bishop on b7 is not taking part in the action. **24 ♘g4 ♘f6 25 ♘xf6 ♗xf6 26 ♖f1 ♕d7 27 f4 a5.** Surely mistimed. Black should play 27 ... ef. After this error White storms the kingside using automatic pilot. **28 f5 ab 29 cb ba 30 ♖f3 ♔g8 31 ♕f2.** The pressure mounts, and Black's extra pawn is totally irrelevant. **31 ... ♗h4 32 ♗xg7 ♗xg3.** If the king takes instead, then 33 ♘h5+ wins. **33 ♖xg3 ♔xg7 34 f6+.** This pawn sticks in Black's gullet like a fishbone. **34 ... ♔h8 35 ♖ga3 ♕b5 36 ♕e3 ♖g8 37 h4 g5.** A desperate last-ditch bid for counterplay. Without it White has the pleasure of choosing whether to attack on the queenside or the kingside. **38 hg ♖g6 39 ♔f2 h6 40 ♖h1 ♔h7 41 ♗d1 ♖ag8 42 ♕h3.** The threat is the queen sacrifice 43 ♕xh6+ ♖xh6 44 ♖xh6 mate. Black's chosen defence does not help at all.

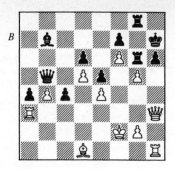

**42 ... ⬛h8 43 ♗h5 1-0.**

Of course, this loss to Sokolov was the exception at Bugojno. More typically, Karpov was the author of some energetic and forceful wins, such as the following game against Spassky, which was undeniably his best in the tournament.

**Karpov-Spassky, Bugojno 1986.** *Ruy Lopez.*
**1 e4 e5 2 ♘f3 ♘c6 3 ♗b5 g6.** An unusual defence favoured by Smyslov and championed by Spassky at the 1985 Montpellier Candidates tournament. **4 c3 a6 5 ♗a4 d6 6 d4 ♗d7 7 0-0 ♗g7 8 ⬛e1 ♘ge7 9 ♗e3 0-0 10 ♘bd2 ♕e8 11 ♗b3 b6.** A curious move that seems to serve no apparent purpose. **12 de de 13 ♘c4 ♔h8 14 ♕c1 ♗g4 15 ♘g5 h6 16 h3.** Counter-attacking the black bishop. White cannot simply withdraw the knight to f3 because 16 ... ♗xf3 shatters his kingside pawns. **16 ... ♗d7 17 ♘f3 ♔h7 18 a4 f5.** Karpov now launches a surprising combination. **19 ef gf 20 ♘cxe5 ♘xe5 21 ♘xe5 ♗xe5 22 ♗xh6.** If now 22 ... ♗g7 then 23 ♗xg7 ♔xg7 24 ♕g5+ wins at once. **22 ... ♗d6 23 ♕g5 ♕g6 24 ⬛xe7+**

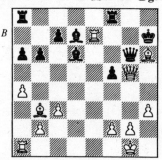

The final phase of the combination, in which White sacrifices rook for bishop but leaves his opponent's king exposed. **24 ... ♗xe7 25 ♕xe7+ ♔xh6 26 ♕xd7 f4**. Spassky would have had a better chance of survival by exchanging queens after 26 ... ♕d6 27 ♕xd6 cd 28 ♖d1, or 27 ♖d1 ♕xd7 28 ♖xd7. **27 ♕xc7 ♖ae8 28 ♖d1 ♖f6 29 ♔h2 a5 30 ♖d4 ♖ef8 31 ♖d7 ♖c6 32 ♕e5**. White is now dominating the board. **32 ... ♕f6 33 ♕d5 ♖c5 34 ♕e4 1-0**. 34 ... ♕g6 35 ♕e7 ♖e8 36 ♕h4+ followed by ♕xf4+ is hopeless for Black.

# 5 The Battle Begins

On the morning of Saturday 19 July a group of chess officials, journalists and photographers waited expectantly at Heathrow's Terminal 2 for the event that would trigger the final countdown to the 1986 centenary world championship match.

First through the barrier were Kasparov's chief second GM Josif Dorfman and his colleagues GM Gennady Timoshchenko and IM Eugene Vladimirov. A couple of minutes later they were followed by World Champion Gary Kasparov and his mother Klara, who chatted with IM Alexander Nikitin and close aide Viktor Litvinov.

As Kasparov was presented with small bouquets of flowers by Leah, 4-year-old daughter of match hospitality officer Adrienne Radford, and Sophie, 5-year-old daughter of world championship press chief Jane Krivine, a third group of Soviets came into the arrivals area.

While greetings were exchanged, Kasparov said "I am very happy to be here in London" and added "I want to say that I am feeling very good".

After politely refusing requests for a quick game from a group of Finnish tourists, Kasparov and his delegation were whisked away and driven to the secret address in central London which was to serve as Kasparov's HQ during the first half of the match.

Over lunch at the house with the authors and a number of match officials, Kasparov revealed that he would be playing football and badminton for relaxation during his stay in London, but refused to be drawn into a discussion on the match itself.

Two days later Karpov and his delegation, which included seconds GM Igor Zaitsev, GM Sergei Makarichev and IM Valery Salov, arrived in London. Karpov was welcomed by match officials and driven to another secret London address for a champagne supper.

At the end of the week both players had a chance to talk publicly about the match at separate press conferences arranged at the Park Lane Hotel, attended by over three hundred journalists and camera crews from Britain, Germany and Brazil.

Neither participant would comment about any personal animosities or the arguments which had flared up between the World Champion and FIDE officials. Kasparov declared that "although I stand by all of my previous statements, the coming months will see our battles resolved over the chessboard and not by a war of words".

Karpov stressed that rivalry was natural between the two best players in the world and stated that when differences do arise "they are of a very temporary nature".

Published and televised reports of the press conference commended the players for their unprecedented charitable gesture of giving all the match winnings to the Chernobyl Relief Fund, set up to aid the victims of the world's worst nuclear disaster. The gift amounts to £300,000 from London, matched by a similar amount from Leningrad. Campomanes announced, though, that the previously imposed tax on each drawn game of 1% of the prize fund would still be payable to FIDE. In the course of another dispute with the organisers over payments to FIDE, Campomanes actually threatened to take down Save & Prosper's nameboard with his bare hands. The sign, sandwiched between the legs of the table on the stage, was immediately nailed down by the organisers, who affixed another similar sign at the back of the table to prevent Campomanes' turning the table around.

Public interest in the match was immense. Most newspapers carried stories about the start and would also later report on the progress of the games. One major breakthrough in press coverage was the tremendous amount of television interest. The BBC continued with their traditional weekly programme about the contest, but Thames TV took the innovative decision to televise a programme about an hour and a half after every game. Within days of the opening, popular demand had led to a repeat of the Thames programme on the mornings following each game.

The arrival of Kasparov and Karpov in London also captured the imagination of nightclub owner Peter Stringfellow, who invited the match organisers and the cast of the *Chess* musical to meet at a party held at the *Hippodrome* in Leicester Square.

## THE OPENING CEREMONY

The Centenary World Championship started on 28 July amidst a fanfare of publicity and spectacle. The Prime Minister, Mrs Margaret Thatcher,

31

opened the match in a stunning ceremony in the Grand Ballroom of the Park Lane Hotel, co-ordinated by Major Michael Parker, fresh from his triumphant staging of the Royal Tournament at Earls Court.

With the floor of the ballroom transformed into a chessboard, decorated at each corner with a giant rook, 500 guests dressed in black and white enjoyed a champagne and caviar reception sponsored by Duncan Lawrie, with fanfares from the band of the Coldstream Guards.

The Prime Minister, dressed in a black two-piece with matching black and white blouse, was escorted through the hall by match organiser Ray Keene. Mrs Thatcher stopped to chat with a number of the guests before making her way to the front of the stage to join the protagonists.

In her speech, greeted with cheering and loud applause from the appreciative chess audience, the Prime Minister noted that she had been presented with a chess set by Soviet Foreign Minister Eduard Shevardnadze on his visit to London earlier in the month. "I give him full marks for diplomacy – the chess set is in fact in blue and white", she added.

Mrs Thatcher also praised the gains made by chess in Britain in recent years and listed the qualities necessary to become a leading chessplayer. The list included precision of thought, imagination and being in good physical shape. Mrs Thatcher added that these characteristics were also those that made a good politician, but added that chess "is limited in time – we deal in unfinished business".

The first speaker, David Jarrett, President of the British Chess Federation, had warmly welcomed the Prime Minister and concluded his address with a line from the musical *Chess*: "Nobody's on nobody's side", referring to the neutrality of the BCF on the match.

Next to be introduced by compère Jeremy James of the BBC's *Master Game* was FIDE President Florencio Campomanes, who began by commenting on the major contribution made by the BCF to "the cause of world chess", both past and present. He went on to say that the Soviet chess authorities "understood the feeling in FIDE that the world championship match belongs to all of FIDE and in the spirit of *gens una sumus* they agreed that the match should be split, with the honours of the opening going abroad." Finally he extended his warmest greetings to both the players.

Alexander Sereda, Deputy Chairman of the Soviet Sports Committee, stressed that the match concluded a "month of co-operation" between the UK and the USSR, including the visit of Shevardnadze and the tour by the Bolshoi Ballet.

After the speeches Kasparov and Karpov joined Mrs Thatcher on stage, where two rooks representing the Tower of London and St Basil's Cathedral in Red Square were located on separate corners. Mrs Thatcher then conducted the drawing of lots by pulling a lever on the first model to reveal two envelopes, one of which was chosen by Karpov. The Prime Minister then repeated the process on the other side for Kasparov. She then announced that Karpov had drawn the white pieces in the first game.

Tim Rice, Honorary Vice-President of the BCF, ended the ceremony by presenting an antique British chess set dating from the 1840s to the Prime Minister.

Karpov's press attaché, Yugoslav journalist Dmitrije Bjelica, said that the evening was "the best and most exciting that I have seen in 30 years of world championships and chess events". Karpov praised the match officials for staging a "wonderful start to the championship".

Among the guests at the reception were the Soviet Ambassador, Leonid Zamyatin, and Peter Pitt, former chair of Arts and Recreation at the GLC. Also present were representatives of the commercial British sponsors and Lincoln Lucena of Brazil, the BCF's favoured candidate for the FIDE presidency. Elaine Paige from *Chess* accompanied Tim Rice, and five other English grandmasters also attended – Short, Plaskett, Stean, Speelman and Mestel.

Jeremy Hanley, MP for Richmond and Barnes, remarked that "this is a tremendous moment for British chess" and stressed that "I'm sure the Prime Minister agreed to take part in the opening because there is no better step on the road to détente with the Soviet Union than a mutual appreciation of the greatest sport in the world".

As she was leaving the ceremony, Mrs Thatcher observed that chess "is rather like mathematics . . . you need to learn it young to get used to it and get it into your bloodstream". She also noted that young people take to chess and computing more quickly than adults.

There is undoubtedly a link between the skills needed for chess and those needed for maths and computer studies. This has not gone unnoticed by chess experts, who have long been advocating that if chess were systematically taught in British schools it would encourage the development of those skills necessary for success in the new computer-related technologies.

## THE FIRST GAME

Early on 28 July a large crowd gathered on Piccadilly outside the Park Lane hotel to await the players' arrival, but both grandmasters preferred to enter through the back of the hotel and avoid the excited onlookers. First to arrive was Karpov in a blue Mercedes. A few minutes later a cream-coloured Ford drew up and Kasparov emerged with his seconds.

Meanwhile, inside the playing hall the whole area in front of the stage was choc-a-bloc with photographers and camera crews. Some reporters even tried to take over the arbiters' area on the right side of the stage.

Kasparov emerged first, followed 30 seconds later by Karpov. After a few words from Match Administrator David Anderton, George Walden MP, the Minister of State for Higher Education, whose portfolio includes chess, made Karpov's opening move.

Two days before the start of the game a suitable chair had not been found for Kasparov. Although Karpov had accepted the beige swivel-chair provided by the organisers, Kasparov had wanted something more austere, and eventually the hotel was able to provide a green upholstered chair. German science writer Friedrich Friedel explained that Kasparov had found the first chair "too comfortable".

The game was played in front of a capacity crowd, who for the first time in a world match were able to watch the moves as soon as they were played on video monitors throughout the hotel, including the press room, the organisers' office and the hotel lounge, where hotel residents and chess fans could sip tea and keep an eye on the progress of the game. This remarkable new system was developed for the BCF by Kevin O'Connell and David Levy, the 'electronic wizards' behind *Intelligent Chess Software*. They devised chessboards and pieces which, amazingly, registered the moves instantaneously on the monitors, thus revolutionising chess as a spectator sport. Their electronics were first used at the GLC London tournament in March 1986, and Grandmasters Spassky and Larsen commented favourably on the abolition of board boys, who had previously moved pieces manually on huge demonstration boards, sometimes dropping pieces, making mistakes or even falling asleep. At the World Championship giant video screens were also placed on either side of the stage, which obviated the common complaint of time scrambles ruining the move demonstration. The moves also appeared on screens in the commentary room, where grandmasters such as Short, Miles and Sosonko were able to analyse the up-to-date positions and demonstrate variations on a parallel screen.

# LONDON

## GAME ONE, 28 July

With 25 minutes to go before play begins the ballroom of the Park Lane
Hotel is crammed to breaking point. Journalists hang over the press
balconies while in front of the stage there are so many photographers
and camera crews that the arbiters' area is invaded.

Five minutes later Kasparov's new chair is brought in and the photographers begin to push and shove for position. Meanwhile, as hundreds
of onlookers wait patiently on Piccadilly for their arrival the players
sneak into the hotel through the back entrance on Brick Street.

Kasparov enters the hall first, dressed in an elegant white suit, and is
followed on to the stage shortly after by Karpov, who is clad in light blue.
Both players receive loud ovations and shake hands. Minister for Higher
Education George Walden comes over to play the opening move, and
the Centenary World Championship begins.

Prior to the start of play bulletin editor Maxim Dlugy, the reigning
World Junior Champion, is already working. He asks Kasparov's
seconds about the first move. Vladimirov predicts 1 e4, while Dorfman
expects 1 d4.

Dorfman gets it right and there is a hum of excitement as Kasparov
moves ... g6, producing his first surprise on the second move. Some
grandmasters murmur "King's Indian", but on move 3 Kasparov flicks
out ... d5, playing the Grünfeld Defence for the first time in his tournament
or match career.

Karpov avoids the sharper continuations, saving such lines for home
analysis. And when the queens are exchanged at move 12 everybody
begins to predict the draw, which Karpov offers after his 21st move.
Some spectators appear a trifle disappointed by the peaceful conclusion
from the sharp, double-edged opening. But 24 games are 24 games, and
Karpov will have time in the future to test out more dangerous variations.
In any case, on the first day the honours go to Kasparov for drawing
effortlessly with Black.

*Cumulative times, in minutes, are shown after each move. Players have 150
minutes each for their first 40 moves and 60 minutes per 16 moves thereafter.*

## Karpov-Kasparov
### *Grünfeld Defence*

| 1 | d4 | ' 00 |
|---|----|----|

Although Karpov is considered essentially an e4 player rather than a d4 adherent, he has not beaten Kasparov with 1 e4 since the third game of their first match! On the contrary, with 1 d4 he has scored no less than five wins over the course of their two earlier clashes. The former champion has probably been deterred from 1 e4 by the porcupine resilience of the Scheveningen Sicilian – so there was a general belief that 1 d4 would be Karpov's main weapon for London, if not Leningrad too.

| 1 | ... | ♘f6 | 01 |
|---|-----|------|-----|
| 2 | c4 | 00 g6 | 01 |
| 3 | ♘c3 | 04 d5 | 01 |

A buzz of excitement went round the audience when Kasparov played this move. This was the first time that he had played the Grünfeld against Karpov in a world championship match. Why the Grünfeld? Kasparov has rarely employed it before, having formerly been an acolyte of the King's Indian, Benoni, Tarrasch and (reluctantly) the Orthodox Defence to the Queen's Gambit. The answer must be that the Grünfeld can only seriously be threatened by sharp, risky attacking lines such as the Exchange Variation (4 cd). In Kasparov's assessment

Karpov would be unwilling to enter such razor-edge opening variations – therefore the Grünfeld is an ideal and surprising choice.

| 4 | ♘f3 | 05 ♗g7 | 01 |
|---|-----|---------|-----|
| 5 | ♗f4 | 10 | |

Karpov beat Korchnoi with 5 ♗g5 at London 1984, but the move is not considered to pose Black serious theoretical problems.

| 5 | ... | c5 | 07 |
|---|-----|----|-----|

Heading for equality. The game which might have acted as a warning to Karpov was played in a simultaneous display in Hamburg on 23 December 1985. That game had gone 5 ... 0-0 6 e3 c5 7 dc ♘e4 8 ♕b3 ♘a6 9 cd ♘axc5 10 ♕c4 b5! 11 ♘xb5 ♗xb2 12 ♗c7 a6!! 13 ♗xd8 ab 14 ♕c2 ♗c3+ 15 ♕xc3 ♘xc3 16 ♗xe7 ♘b3 17 ♖d1 ♖xa2 18 ♗xf8 ♔xf8 19 ♘d4 ♘xd1 20 ♘xb3 ♘xf2 and Black went on to win (Bernhorst-Kasparov). This was the famous clock simul where Grandmaster Murray Chandler was one of Kasparov's opponents.

| 6 | dc | 11 ♕a5 | 07 |
|---|----|---------|-----|

| | | | |
|---|---|---|---|
| 7 | **≅c1** *21* | | |

After ten minutes thought. It is hardly a shock that Karpov, who could not have been expecting the Grünfeld, avoids the colossal complications of 7 cd ♘xd5 8 ♕xd5 ♗xc3+ 9 ♗d2 ♗e6. In his excellent bulletin notes Dlugy quoted a game Dreev-Yepishin, Tallinn 1986: 10 ♕xb7 ♗xd2+ 11 ♘xd2 0-0 12 e4 ♘c6! 13 ♕a6 ♕xc5 14 ♕b5 ♕d6 15 ♘c4 ♕d4 16 ♗e2 ≅fc8 17 0-0 ≅ab8 18 ♕a4 ♕xe4 19 ≅fe1 ♘d4 20 ♗f1 ♕f4 21 b3 ≅c5 22 ♕xa7 ≅h5 23 h3 ≅xh3 24 ♕xb8 ♕xb8 25 gh ♘f3+ 26 ♔g2 ♗d5 0-1.

| | | | |
|---|---|---|---|
| 7 | ... | **dc** | *12* |
| 8 | **e3** *21* | **♕xc5** | *16* |
| 9 | **♕a4+** *23* | | |

White's opening has not been a resounding success. Now he has to look for ways to regain his pawn. Dlugy even suggested that Black might try here 9 ... ♗d7!? 10 ♕xc4 ♕b6 11 ♘b5 ♘a6 12 ♗c7 ♕e6 as an active way of playing.

| | | | |
|---|---|---|---|
| 9 | ... | **♘c6** | *34* |
| 10 | **♗xc4** *44* | **0-0** | *36* |
| 11 | **0-0** *48* | **♗d7** | *48* |
| 12 | **♕b5** *75* | | |

Karpov has evidently decided to opt for a draw. If 12 ♗e2 or 12 ♘b5, seeking to retain some tension in the position, then 12 ... ♕b4! equalises in both cases.

| | | | |
|---|---|---|---|
| 12 | ... | **♕xb5** | *51* |
| 13 | **♗xb5** *76* | **≅ac8** | *74* |
| 14 | **≅fd1** *79* | **≅fd8** | *75* |
| 15 | **h3** *80* | | |

Creating an escape for his QB should it be threatened by ... ♘h5.

| | | | |
|---|---|---|---|
| 15 | ... | **h6!** | *90* |

A similar notion. Black wants to be able to station his queen's bishop on e6 without fearing ♘g5.

| | | | |
|---|---|---|---|
| 16 | **♔f1** *88* | **a6** | *95* |
| 17 | **♗e2** *91* | **♗e6** | *98* |
| 18 | **≅xd8+** *101* | | |

After 18 ♘e5 ♘b4 19 a3 ♘bd5 20 ♘xd5 ♘xd5 21 ♗g3 ≅xc1 22 ≅xc1 ≅c8 23 ≅xc8+ ♗xc8 24 ♗f3 ♗e6 the position looks dead equal.

| | | | |
|---|---|---|---|
| 18 | ... | **≅xd8** | *98* |
| 19 | **♘e5** *103* | **♘xe5** | *103* |
| 20 | **♗xe5** *103* | **≅d2** | *108* |
| 21 | **b3** *107* | | |

**Draw Agreed**

If 21 ... ♘d5 22 ♗xg7 ♔xg7 23 ≅d1! ≅xd1+ 24 ♘xd1 ♘b4 25 ♘c3.

| | |
|---|---|
| **Kasparov** | ½ |
| **Karpov** | ½ |

# GAME TWO, 30-31 July

With memories in the back of everyone's mind of his victory with White in game 1 of their 1985 match, Kasparov outplays the Challenger in an ending, only to miss an easy victory at move 39.

Game 2 gave Karpov his first opportunity to produce a TN, and Kasparov pondered for 44 minutes wondering what to do. In the end he found a way to keep a small but enduring edge and outmanoeuvred Karpov in a risk-free position with a symmetrical pawn structure. As onlookers gathered round the video screens in the press and grandmaster rooms Kasparov's winning continuation was shouted again and again. But with four minutes remaining on his clock Kasparov stunned the crowd by playing his move almost instantly, letting an immediate and clear victory slip away. Karpov surely couldn't believe his good fortune, though when the game was adjourned Kasparov retained his pawn advantage. Initial assessments of the position gave the Champion very good winning chances.

Half an hour after play had ended a group of grandmasters gathered in the press room, feverishly analysing the position. Eventually Dutch GM Gennady Sosonko and America's Lubosh Kavalek concluded that the position was in fact no easy win.

When play resumed Karpov was able to hold on to the draw, though some experts were sure that Kasparov must have missed a win somewhere in his overnight analysis. Indeed after the game Karpov's press attaché Dmitrije Bjelica rushed into the press room to make a statement on Karpov's behalf, reflecting the Challenger's improved attitude towards the press. Karpov's view was that the adjourned position had been a 50/50 balance between a win for White and a draw.

### Kasparov-Karpov
*NImzo-Indian Defence*

| | | | | |
|---|---|---|---|---|
| 1 | d4 | 00 | ♘f6 | 00 |
| 2 | c4 | 00 | e6 | 00 |
| 3 | ♘c3 | 01 | ♝b4 | 00 |

Karpov used to be considered invulnerable in the Nimzo-Indian and I (RDK) well remember the difficulties we had trying to break it down during the 1978 match in Baguio when I was Korchnoi's chief second.

**4 ♘f3 _01_**

But against this harmless-looking developing move Karpov has recently appeared to be remarkably helpless. Kasparov wrote: "Revealing . . . is the creative debate in the Nimzo-Indian . . . Karpov experienced serious difficulties in this opening. The strategic pattern obviously did not appeal to him, and it was precisely this factor that we had taken into account in our preparations."

**4 ... c5 _07_**

**5 g3 _01_**

See also the comments to the Nimzo-Indian in game 4.

**5 ... ♘c6 _09_**

**6 ♗g2 _02_ d5 _11_**

Nevertheless, Karpov springs his innovation first, and Kasparov went into an immense huddle.

**7 cd _46_**

If 7 0-0?! dc 8 dc ♕e7 9 ♘d2 0-0 10 ♘xc4 ♕xc5 = (Dlugy).

**7 ... ♘xd5 _12_**

**8 ♗d2! _47_**

At first sight a paradoxical choice, since White's centre appears to be underprotected, but a neat, typically Kasparovian, tactical trick keeps White slightly on top.

**8 ... cd _16_**

**9 ♘xd4 _48_ ♘xd4 _27_**

Or 9 ... ♗xc3 10 bc ♘de7 11 ♗f4! (Sosonko) – a line that anticipates game 4.

**10 ♘xd5 _48_**

Here White regains his material and ends up with nagging pressure along the h1-a8 diagonal from his "Catalan" bishop on g2.

**10 ... ♗xd2+ _28_**

**11 ♕xd2 _48_ ♘c6 _40_**

11 ... ♘f5 is also playable, but 11 ... ed 12 ♕xd4 does not come into consideration.

**12 ♘f4 _78_**

Heading for an endgame where the white knight will rest on c5. Other ideas are 12 ♘e3 ♕xd2+ 13 ♔xd2 ♗e7 14 ♖hd1 ♖d8+ 15 ♔c3 ♗d7 16 ♘c4 ♗e8 17 b4 ± or 12 ♕e3 0-0 13 ♘c3 ♗d7 14 0-0 ♕e7 15 ♘e4 – also ±.

**12 ... ♕xd2+ _40_**

In this match Karpov rarely passes over any opportunity to trade queens, an interesting psychological characteristic, reminiscent of Botvinnik's strategy in his 1961 revenge match against Tal.

**13 ♔xd2 _78_ ♗d7 _40_**

**14 ♖hc1 _78_ ♔e7 _45_**

**15 ♘d3 _81_ ♖hc8 _80_**

Not 15 ... ♖hd8 16 ♘c5 ♗e8+ 17 ♔e1 b6 18 ♘xe6! ±.

**16 ♘c5    93    ♖ab8    85**

This may be too passive. Perhaps 16 ... b6 17 ♘xd7 (17 ♘a6 ♖d8! 18 ♔e1 ♖ac8) 17 ... ♔xd7 18 ♖c3 ♖c7 19 ♖ac1 ♖ac8, which looks tenable, as given by IM Polovodin in the special Leningrad bulletin produced there by the M.I.Chigorin Club.

**17 ♖c3    101    ♘d8    88**
**18 ♖ac1    104**

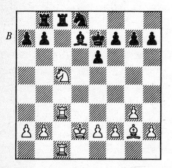

Kasparov builds up the pressure, step by step. Black now has another chance to throw off his shackles with 18 ... b6, but two moves later it looks less reliable, viz 19 ♘xd7 ♔xd7 20 ♖d3+ ♔e7 21 ♖a3 a5 22 b4 ♖xc1 23 ♔xc1 ab 24 ♖a7+ followed by ♔b2 and ♔b3.

| 18 | ... | | ♗c6 | 102 |
|----|-----|----|-----|-----|
| 19 | ♘d3 | 105 | ♗d7 | 106 |
| 20 | ♘e5 | 107 | ♖xc3 | 108 |
| 21 | ♖xc3 | 109 | ♗e8 | 110 |
| 22 | b4 | 110 | a6 | 112 |
| 23 | ♗e4 | 116 | | |

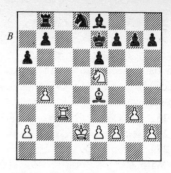

Dlugy recommends instead here 23 a3 a5 24 ba ♖a8 25 ♖c5 ♔d6 26 ♘d3 ♗c6 27 e4.

Karpov has often been bracketed with Capablanca, Kasparov with Alekhine. At his pre-match press conference Karpov rejected this view, but time and again parallels between Kasparov's play and Alekhine's crop up. Remember, Alekhine was not just a dynamic-revolutionary-sacrificial maniac, he was also capable of iron-hard strategic and positional chess in simplified positions. Compare, for instance, the diagrammed position with Alekhine-Euwe, match (24) Rotterdam 1937: 1 ♘f3 d5 2 c4 e6 3 d4 ♘f6 4 ♘c3 c5 5 cd ♘xd5 6 g3 cd 7 ♘xd5 ♕xd5 8 ♕xd4 ♕xd4 9 ♘xd4 ♗b4+ 10 ♗d2 ♗xd2+ 11 ♔xd2 ♔e7? (11 ... ♗d7 12 ♗g2 ♘c6! Alekhine) 12 ♗g2 ♖d8 13 ♔e3 ♘a6 14 ♖ac1 ♖b8 15 a3 ♗d7 16 f4 f6 17 ♗e4 ♗e8 18 b4! and after solving various technical problems White went on to win.

40

| 23 | ... | | h6 | 114 |
|----|-----|---|-----|-----|
| 24 | a3 | 121 | f6? | 131 |

After the game Karpov said to us that 24 ... a5! equalises, e.g. 25 ba ♖a8 26 ♖c5 ♔d6 27 ♘d3 ♗c6. Now the ex-Champion has to suffer . . .

| 25 | ♘d3 | 127 | ♗c6 | 131 |
|----|-----|-----|-----|-----|
| 26 | ♗xc6 | 128 | ♘xc6 | 131 |
| 27 | ♘c5 | 128 | | |

With threats such as ♘xa6 or ♘xb7, annihilating the foundations of Black's knight.

| 27 | ... | | ♘e5 | 132 |
|----|-----|---|-----|-----|

If 27 ... ♘a7 then still 28 ♘xa6! ba 29 ♖c7+. Polovodin gives, as a final attempt to break out of the steadily tightening straitjacket, 27 ... a5!? 28 ♖d3 ♘e5 29 ♖d4 ab, or 28 b5 ♘d4 29 ♖d3 b6. Ingenious, but Black is walking a tightrope.

| 28 | f4 | 129 | ♘d7 | 132 |
|----|-----|-----|-----|-----|
| 29 | ♘b3 | 130 | ♔d6 | 135 |

If 29 ... f5 30 ♘d4 ♔d6 31 ♖d3 ♔e7 32 ♖e3. A better defence is afforded by 30 ... g6 31 ♖e3 ♘f8, even though it is hideously passive.

| 30 | e4 | 131 | | |
|----|-----|-----|---|---|

White encroaches on yet more territory.

| 30 | ... | | g5 | 139 |
|----|-----|---|-----|-----|

Striving to fight back.

| 31 | ♔e3 | 136 | e5 | 144 |
|----|-----|-----|-----|-----|

It is difficult to believe that the hyper-solid, super-positional Karpov is the progenitor of this move, which simultaneously sacrifices his influence over the key

squares d5 and f5. Alternatives, however, are out of stock, e.g. 31 ... b6? 32 ♘d4! or 31 ... gf+ 32 gf e5 33 ♘a5 ef+ 34 ♔xf4, or in this line 32 ... ♖g8 33 ♘a5 ♖g2 34 ♘xb7+ ♔e7 35 ♖c7! winning, much as could later have transpired in the game.

| 32 | fg | 143 | fg | 144 |
|----|-----|-----|-----|-----|

If 32 ... hg 33 ♔f3! with regal light-square penetration soon to come.

| 33 | ♘a5 | 143 | | |
|----|-----|-----|---|---|

Black, tied to b7, is now effectively in "volkswagen", as they say in Germany.

| 33 | ... | | g4 | 145 |
|----|-----|---|-----|-----|
| 34 | ♖c2 | 143 | h5 | 146 |
| 35 | ♖c1 | 144 | b6 | 147 |

Desperation. Karpov hates to play moves this weakening, even if they do not lose by force, which in fact 35 ... b6 does. However, 35 ... ♘f6 36 ♖c5 ♘d7 37 ♘c4+ ♔e6 38 ♖c7 is also utterly hopeless for Black.

| 36 | ♖c6+ | 146 | ♔e7 | 147 |
|----|------|-----|-----|-----|

41

| 37 | ♘c4 | *146* | ♖f8 | *148* |
|----|------|-------|------|-------|
| 38 | ♔e2 | *146* | ♖f3 | *148* |

Or 38 ... ♖f6 39 ♖c7 ♔e6 40 ♖a7.

**39 ♘e3?? *146***

Very natural, and played quickly – yet a super-colossal blunder. We have heard that Kasparov smote his head with his hands when seconds pointed out 39 ♖c7! to him shortly after adjournment.

The variations are simplicity itself:

a) 39 ... ♔e6 40 ♖xd7 ♔xd7 41 ♘xe5+;

b) 39 ... ♖b3 40 ♘xb6 ♔d6 41 ♖xd7+ ♔c6 42 ♖d3 ♖b2+ 43 ♖d2;

c) 39 ... ♖c3 40 ♔d2 etc;

d) 39 ... ♖f6 40 ♘xe5 ♔d6 41 ♘xd7 ♖f7 42 ♖a7.

**39 ... ♘f6 *148***

Karpov now stages a remarkable comeback.

| 40 | ♖xb6 | *147* | ♘xe4 | *149* |
|----|------|-------|------|-------|
| 41 | ♖xa6 | *150* | | |

A besetting sin with Kasparov,

and a surprising one, considering the iron discipline of his mentor Botvinnik – he does not seal early enough! Here "seals move" is the best, giving Karpov 41 ♘d5+ to analyse as well. Probably, though, Black would be able to hang on after 41 ... ♔f7 42 ♖xa6 h4 43 gh ♖h3.

**41 ... ♖f2+ *156***

The sealed move. The adjourned position was proclaimed lost by Dlugy, Short, Sosonko and many others. Co-author Keene in the Thames TV slot predicted "blood on the sand". Only wily, experienced old fox Kavalek pronounced "very hard to win". He was right, and after overnight analysis his view had become the consensus.

| 42 | ♔d3 | *150* | ♘d6 | *156* |
|----|------|-------|------|-------|
| 43 | ♖a7+ | *152* | | |

Or 43 a4 ♖xh2 and now:

a) 44 ♖a7+ ♔e6 45 ♖h7 e4+ 46 ♔c3 (46 ♔d4 ♖d2+ 47 ♔c5 ♖d3) 46 ... ♖e2 47 ♖h6+ ♔d7 48 ♘c4 ♘xc4 49 ♔xc4 ♖e3 50 ♖xh5 ♖xg3 = – analysis by Dlugy in the bulletin.

b) 44 b5 ♖a2 45 ♖a7+ (45 b6 ♔d7-c6) 45 ... ♔e6 46 b6 ♖a3+ 47 ♔e2 ♖a2+ (48 ♔d3 ♖a3+ 49 ♔d2 ♘e4+ 50 ♔c2 ♖xe3 51 b7 ♖e2+ 52 ♔d3 ♖b2 53 ♔xe4 h4!).

| 43 | ... | | ♔e6 | *157* |
|----|-----|---|------|-------|
| 44 | ♖h7 | *153* | e4+ | *160* |

Not 44 ... ♖xh2 45 ♖h6+ ♔e7 46 a4!.

**45  &c3**   *165*

If 45 &d4 we enter the last truly critical variation:

a) **45 ...  Id2+** 46 &c5 Id3 and now:

a1) **47 &g2?!** Ic3+ 48 &b6 &c8+.

a2) **47 Ih6+!** &d7 48 &g2 (48 &d5 &b7+ 49 &c4 &d6+) 48 ... Ic3+ 49 &d5! (49 &b6Ic6+ 50 &a5 &b7+ or 50 &a7 &c8+) 49 ... Id3+ 50 &e5 Id2 51 Ih7+ &c6 52 &e3 and White should win.

b) **45 .. Ixh2!** followed by ... Id2+ and ... Id3 should be sufficient. If 46 &xg4 Id2+!.

**45  ...  &b5+!**   *161*

Here 45 ... Ixh2? 46 Ih6+ followed by 47 &xg4 does cause problems for Black since he no longer has the resource ... Id2+.

**46  &c4**   *167*

If 46 &b3 If3 47 Ih6+ &d7 48 &c4 Ixe3 49 &xb5 Ixa3 50 Ixh5 e3 51 Ie5 &d6.

| | | | |
|---|---|---|---|
| **46** | ... | &xa3+ | *162* |
| **47** | **&d4** | *170* | Ixh2 | *163* |
| **48** | **Ih6+** | *177* | &d7 | *188* |
| **49** | **&d5** | *187* | h4! | *206* |

Throwing a spanner in the works of the initiative White hoped for with rook and knight co-operating against the black king.

**50  Ixh4**   *202*

Or 50 gh g3.

| | | | |
|---|---|---|---|
| **50** | ... | Ixh4 | *206* |
| **51** | **gh** | *202* | g3 | *206* |
| **52** | **&f4** | *202* | | |

52 &e3 &c2+!.

**52  ...  &c2+**   *206*

**Draw Agreed**

53 &c3 &e3 54 &d4 g2 55 &h3 &f5+.

One of the "ones that got away".

| | | | |
|---|---|---|---|
| **Kasparov** | ½ | ½ | 1 |
| **Karpov** | ½ | ½ | 1 |

# GAME THREE, 1 August

Kasparov holds with the Grünfeld Defence for the second time, by playing a solid equalising line against Karpov's fianchetto variation. Karpov moved quickly in the opening, but despite having more than half an hour in hand on the clock he was unable to achieve any substantial advantage.

Although this game lasted far longer than the first, the general feeling was that Karpov was getting nowhere with White. After playing his 35th move in a dead equal position Karpov offered a draw which was accepted immediately.

Despite the draws chess continues to hit the headlines. Canadian pundit and Albert Einstein lookalike Nathan Divinsky had the rare honour of appearing on *Wogan*, Britain's premier chat show, not once but twice in a row. Divinsky's interviews followed those of Nigel Short and Gary Kasparov in March and June – four appearances by chessplayers in less than six months. In the bulletin Nigel Davies joked that it would soon be a case of Wogan appearing on *Divinsky*.

### Karpov-Kasparov
*Grünfeld Defence*

| 1 | d4 | 00 | ♘f6 | 00 |
| 2 | c4 | 00 | g6 | 00 |
| 3 | ♘f3 | 05 | | |

Evidently Karpov is not yet ready to engage in a full-blooded Grünfeld theoretical dispute. He steers for a quiet system with which he enjoyed recent success against Timman.

| 3 | ... | | ♗g7 | 00 |
| 4 | g3 | 05 | c6 | 02 |

Kasparov had already tried a Schlechter-Grünfeld in game 2 of his Miles match, so this super-solid system can hardly have come as a shock.

| 5 | ♗g2 | 06 | d5 | 02 |
| 6 | cd | 06 | | |

The alternative here is 6 ♘bd2. White's choice tends towards equality but is not without sting.

| 6 | ... | | cd | 02 |
| 7 | ♘c3 | 06 | 0-0 | 03 |
| 8 | ♘e5 | 07 | e6 | 06 |
| 9 | 0-0 | 07 | | |

In Karpov-Timman, Bugojno 1986, White tried 9 ♗g5, with the follow-up 9 ... ♕b6 10 ♕d2 ♘fd7 11 ♘f3 ♘c6 12 ♖d1 ♘f6 13 0-0

&d7 14 &xf6 &xf6 15 e4. Karpov
won, but Timman's position was
defensible for a long time. Further-
more, 13 ... ♘e4!? comes into
consideration as an improvement.

| 9 | ... | | ♘fd7 | 06 |
|---|---|---|---|---|
| 10 | ♘f3 | 10 | ♘c6 | 07 |
| 11 | ♗f4 | 10 | ♘f6 | 21 |
| 12 | ♘e5 | 14 | | |

The marches and countermarches
of the black and white knights are
apparently bemusing but in the
end logically justifiable. In the
game Podgayets-Marsalek, USSR
1974, White temporised with 12
♖c1 ♕e7 13 ♕d2 ♗d7, but then
decided that the time had come
and at last opted for 14 ♘e5.

| 12 | ... | | ♗d7 | 29 |
|---|---|---|---|---|
| 13 | ♕d2 | 15 | ♘xe5 | 46 |
| 14 | ♗xe5 | 18 | | |

Kasparov looked visibly relieved
after this mode of capturing, but
as Dlugy pointed out, if 14 de ♘g4
15 e4 d4! 16 ♕xd4 ♗c6 17 ♕d6
♕b6, with tremendously active
play for the sacrificed pawn.

| 14 | ... | | ♗c6 | 47 |
|---|---|---|---|---|
| 15 | ♖fd1 | 35 | ♘d7 | 68 |
| 16 | ♗xg7 | 42 | ♔xg7 | 70 |
| 17 | ♖ac1 | 42 | ♘f6 | 73 |
| 18 | ♕f4 | 44 | ♕b8 | 75 |
| 19 | ♕xb8 | 49 | | |

We had expected 19 ♕e5 ♕xe5
20 fe ♘g4 21 f4, though Black can
cause trouble with 21 ... ♘e3 or
21 ... g5.

| 19 | ... | | ♖axb8 | 76 |
|---|---|---|---|---|

| 20 | f3 | 55 | ♖fd8 | 85 |
|---|---|---|---|---|

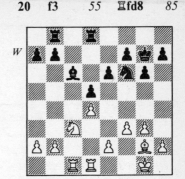

| 21 | ♔f2 | 60 | | |
|---|---|---|---|---|

White cannot carry out his prime
strategic objective, which is e4.
For example, 21 e4 de 22 fe e5! 23
d5 ♗d7. White has a passed pawn,
but his bishop is bad and his
prospects generally sterile. Black
will proceed adventurously with
... ♘e8-d6.

| 21 | ... | | ♖bc8 | 88 |
|---|---|---|---|---|
| 22 | e3 | 62 | ♘e8 | 90 |
| 23 | ♖d2 | 64 | ♘d6 | 91 |
| 24 | ♖dc2 | 65 | ♔f8 | 96 |
| 25 | ♗f1 | 67 | ♔e7 | 103 |
| 26 | ♗d3 | 68 | f5!? | 107 |

This bold move loosens the dark
squares. It caused a minor sensation
amongst the assembled experts.
To us, however, it represents a
natural reaction to clarify matters
and discover whether White really
has any kind of edge.

| 27 | h4 | 74 | h6 | 114 |
|---|---|---|---|---|
| 28 | b3 | 91 | | |

Karpov likes to play this when
his opponent has a knight on b6 or

d6. 28 g4 is more energetic but Black survives after 28 ... ♘f7.

| 28 | ... | | g5 | *118* |
|---|---|---|---|---|
| 29 | ♘e2 | *93* | ♗d7 | *121* |
| 30 | ♖c5 | *94* | b6 | *126* |
| 31 | ♖c7 | *95* | ♖xc7 | *126* |
| 32 | ♖xc7 | *95* | ♖a8! | *126* |

A calm decision. White's rook will soon be expelled.

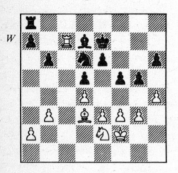

**33 ♘g1?!** *119*

Tantamount to offering a draw. If White can continue it is with Dlugy's idea of 33 hg hg 34 ♗a6!.

The point of this is not so much to control c8 with the bishop as to vacate d3 for the annoying manoeuvre ♘c1-d3. Karpov spent 24 minutes before rejecting this procedure. So how does Black equalise? If 34 ... ♔d8 35 ♖c1! ♔e7 36 ♖h1 and the attack is directed along the h-file. Alternatively, 34 ... ♘e8 35 ~~♖c2~~ (to keep c1 free for the knight) 35 ... ♘d6 36 ♘c1 ♘f7 37 ♘d3 ♔d6 38 f4 g4 39 ♘e5 ♘xe5 40 de+ ♔e7 41 ♖c7 ♔d8 42 ♖b7 ♗c8 43 ♖h7 and White wins. The best defence is 37 ... ♖h8 38 ♔g2 ♔d8, which is just sufficient to repel boarders. If instead 34 ... ♘e8 35 ♖c1 ♘d6 36 ♖h1 ♘f7 followed by ... ♖h8. In any case Karpov had to try this if he wanted to prolong the game.

| 33 | ... | | ♘e8 | *135* |
|---|---|---|---|---|
| 34 | ♖c1 | *120* | ♖c8 | *135* |
| 35 | ♖xc8 | *131* | **Draw Agreed** | |

| Kasparov | ½ ½ ½ | 1½ |
|---|---|---|
| Karpov | ½ ½ ½ | 1½ |

# GAME FOUR, 4 August

After dominating the first three games Kasparov scores a victory in the fourth to take the lead with a brilliant display of aggressive and uncompromising attacking chess.

The first blood came when Karpov adjourned a pawn down in a lost position after being outplayed in the late middlegame. Sensing that the game was over, the crowd gave Kasparov a loud ovation after he sealed his 41st move. And this time grandmasters seemed sure that Karpov would give in. The next day at 3.44 pm Karpov telephoned Lothar Schmid to announce his resignation, and the arbiter made available to journalists copies of the confirming letter.

Kasparov arrived early for this game. The opening – one of Kasparov's special weapons from the '85 match – caused tremendous excitement. Fearing an improvement Karpov diverged from known theory, but he went wrong at move 13, allowing Kasparov to build up a dangerous initiative in the centre. The pressure continued as Kasparov unleashed his bishop pair and doubled on the d-file, eventually penetrating into the heart of Karpov's position to win a pawn. When Karpov was left with only one minute for his last five moves Kasparov supporters, with vivid memories of game 2, became nervous as their man appeared to miss the best continuations. But Kasparov simply threw his a-pawn down the board.

This decisive game was witnessed by Viktor Korchnoi, who descended on London for an interview and to watch the rematch. Also present to swell the ranks of grandmasters was Tony Miles, recently returned from a tournament in Biel, and various players in London to play in the Commonwealth Championship. These included a large delegation of Icelanders and a group of Soviet emigrés, who together with the bilingual Max Dlugy, ensured that English was not always the dominant language in the GM analysis room.

Korchnoi chose to watch the games on the video screens in the hotel lounge. This trend was to become widespread. By the later games the lounge had become a sea of chessplayers discussing the games over coffee. Sensibly enough, though, a decision was made not to place a monitor in the hotel bar.

### Kasparov-Karpov
*Nimzo-Indian Defence*

| 1 | **d4** | *00* | ♘**f6** | *00* |
|---|---|---|---|---|
| 2 | **c4** | *00* | **e6** | *01* |
| 3 | ♘**c3** | *01* | ♗**b4** | *01* |
| 4 | ♘**f3** | *01* | **c5** | *05* |
| 5 | **g3** | *01* | **cd** | *06* |

This transposes into the main lines of the English Opening and avoids the line played in game 2.

| 6 | ♘**xd4** | *01* | **0-0** | *06* |
|---|---|---|---|---|
| 7 | ♗**g2** | *02* | **d5** | *06* |
| 8 | ♕**b3** | *04* | ♗**xc3+** | *07* |
| 9 | **bc** | *04* | ♘**c6** | *09* |

A novelty. The most interesting cross-reference is Karpov-Portisch, Lucerne 1985, where Black played 9 ... dc 10 ♕a3 ♘bd7 11 ♘b5 with an unclear position. This game ended in a draw.

| 10 | **cd** | *06* |
|---|---|---|

Black was threatening ... ♘a5.

| 10 | ... | | ♘**a5** | *11* |
|---|---|---|---|---|

Tony Miles, analysing the game in the *Times* commentary room at the Park Lane Hotel, noted that this was "a move Black will regret for the rest of the game".

| 11 | ♕**c2** | *06* | ♘**xd5** | *16* |
|---|---|---|---|---|
| 12 | ♕**d3!** | *16* | | |

It is highly characteristic of Kasparov's style to disregard pawn structure in favour of more dynamic considerations, such as piece mobility. The weakness evident on the c-file is now traditional in a Kasparov-Karpov Nimzo-Indian.

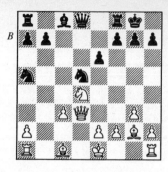

| 12 | ... | | ♗**d7** | *31* |
|---|---|---|---|---|

A firm grip on c4 would give Black the better chances, so White now has to find something against 13 ... ♖c8.

| 13 | **c4!** | *47* | ♘**e7** | *49* |
|---|---|---|---|---|

If 13 ... ♘b4 14 ♕c3 ♘ac6 15 ♗a3 a5 16 ♘b5 is slightly better for White. Or 13 ... ♘b6 14 c5 ♘a4 15 ♗a3 ♗c6 16 ♘xc6 ♘xc6 17 ♕b5 is also in White's favour. Interestingly, Karpov often emerges from his Nimzo-Indians against Kasparov with theoretical equality, but his overall score in the last match and so far in this one is only 2-6!

| 14 | **0-0** | *51* |
|---|---|---|

14 ♗a3!? ♖c8 15 ♖c1 is also slightly better for White.

| 14 | ... | | ♖**c8** | *75* |
|---|---|---|---|---|

If 14 ... e5 then 15 ♘b5 ♗c6 16 ♗a3 again results in a small edge for White.

| 15 | ♘**b3** | *56* | ♘**xc4** | *75* |
|---|---|---|---|---|
| 16 | ♗**xb7** | *56* | ♖**c7** | *75* |
| 17 | ♗**a6!** | *57* | | |

Dlugy called this "brilliant un-stereotyped play" and notes that instead of playing 17 ♗e4 to maintain pressure on the b1-h7 diagonal, which leads nowhere after 17 ... h6, Kasparov "insists on fighting for control of the c4 square. White now plays a game of cat and mouse with Black's pieces, eventually getting them to tread on each others' toes."

| 17 | ... | | ♘e5 | 79 |
|----|-----|-----|-----|-----|
| 18 | ♕e3 | 71 | ♘c4 | 103 |
| 19 | ♕e4! | 85 | | |

If 19 ♗xc4 ♖xc4 20 ♕xa7 ♘d5 Black has compensation for the pawn.

| 19 | ... | | ♘d6?! | 121 |
|----|-----|-----|-----|-----|

Karpov was behind on time and Dlugy considers 19 ... ♕a8! essential, aiming to defend an inferior endgame after 20 ♕xa8 ♖xa8 21 ♗g5 ♘d5 22 ♖fc1 ♘cb6 23 ♗d2!. Kasparov's next move takes them into a version of this.

| 20 | ♕d3 | 101 | ♖c6 | 124 |
|----|-----|-----|-----|-----|
| 21 | ♗a3! | 105 | | |

This late development of the white queen's bishop, which has rejected so many earlier possibilities of leaping into the fray, is reminiscent of Lasker's famous delayed deployment of his QB in the first game with Marshall in 1908.

| 21 | ... | | ♗c8 | 128 |
|----|-----|-----|-----|-----|

21 ... ♕b6 22 ♘c5 ♖xc5 23 ♗xc5 ♕xc5 24 ♖fd1 ♘d5 25 e4 with great advantage. 22 ♘d4 is also murderous.

| 22 | ♗xc8 | 105 | ♘dxc8 | 129 |
|----|-----|-----|-----|-----|
| 23 | ♖fd1 | 112 | ♕xd3 | 130 |
| 24 | ♖xd3 | 112 | ♖e8 | 133 |
| 25 | ♖ad1 | 113 | f6 | 133 |

White's position is dominating. His rooks roam the important d-file at will, while his bishop rakes the entire black camp from its post at a3.

| 26 | ♘d4 | 122 | ♖b6 | 134 |
|----|-----|-----|-----|-----|
| 27 | ♗c5 | 122 | ♖a6 | 135 |
| 28 | ♘b5 | 125 | ♖c6 | 135 |
| 29 | ♗xe7 | 125 | | |

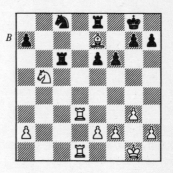

| 29 | ... | | ♘xe7 | 136 |
|----|-----|-----|-----|-----|

49

Dlugy notes that 29 ... ♖xe7 loses at once to 30 ♖d8+ followed by 31 ♖xc8 ♖xc8 32 ♘d6+.

| 30 | ♖d7 | 125 | ♘g6 | 146 |
| 31 | ♖xa7 | 127 | ♘f8 | 146 |
| 32 | a4 | 128 | ♖b8 | 147 |
| 33 | e3 | 130 | h5 | 147 |
| 34 | ♔g2 | 132 | e5 | 148 |

In time pressure Karpov's position crumbles.

| 35 | ♖d3 | 134 | ♔h7 | 149 |
| 36 | ♖c3 | 139 | ♖bc8 | 149 |
| 37 | ♖xc6 | 141 | ♖xc6 | 149 |
| 38 | ♘c7 | 142 | ♘e6 | 149 |
| 39 | ♘d5 | 142 | ♔h6 | 149 |
| 40 | a5 | 143 | e4 | 149 |

The adjourned position. Kasparov sealed **41 a6**, but Karpov **resigned** the following afternoon without resuming play.

| Kasparov | ½ ½ ½ 1 | 2½ |
| Karpov | ½ ½ ½ 0 | 1½ |

50

# GAME FIVE, 6 August

So far, all the running in the match had come from the Champion, but Karpov now hit back at once with a fine victory after out-preparing and then outplaying an incautious Kasparov. And given the Champion's dominance in the first games, it was important for Karpov to break out of the psychological straitjacket immediately.

After his victory in the previous game Kasparov came out of his corner in an aggressive mood, entering a double-edged variation of the Grünfeld Defence which theory considered rather dubious. Karpov built up a huge phalanx of pawns in the centre which Kasparov tried to undermine using an opening novelty. Karpov was able to establish a dangerous passed d-pawn, part of a chain that froze out Kasparov's Grünfeld bishop.

In the commentary room Miles was highly critical of Black's 18th, and the key turning-point came with a subtle knight manoeuvre initiated by White's 20th. John Nunn quickly gauged the position as almost winning for White, and suggested that Kasparov's team had missed this plan during analysis. Speaking after move 22, Viktor Korchnoi said: "Five moves ago I said Black was totally lost, and nothing has changed".

In an effort to gain counterplay Kasparov began to play slowly, eventually sacrificing a pawn but then failing to go down the critical variation. In an ironic counterpoint to game 4 Kasparov hunched over the table and threw his a-pawn down the board in an effort to confuse the issue. But Karpov blocked the pawn on the 7th, and was set to capture it and move on to win a third when the Champion resigned.

Kasparov appeared to take this setback in his stride. He commented later that his team had made an error in analysis, but added that at least it had occurred at an early stage in the match and was unlikely to be repeated. Kasparov also took the extremely sensible course of having a time-out after this bruising. After losses in the 6th game of the 84/85 match and in the 4th of their second title bout Kasparov had failed to take a time-out after a bad loss. On both occasions he went on to lose the next game as well.

The match was once again wide open.

### Karpov-Kasparov
*Grünfeld Defence*

| 1 | d4 | 00 | ♘f6 | 00 |
|---|----|----|----|----|
| 2 | c4 | 00 | g6 | 00 |
| 3 | ♘c3 | 01 | d5 | 01 |
| 4 | ♗f4 | 01 | ♗g7 | 01 |
| 5 | e3 | 02 | c5 | 05 |

5 ... 0-0 6 cd ♘xd5 7 ♘xd5 ♕xd5 8 ♗xc7 is quite in Kasparov's style, but the whole gambit line was dealt a hideous blow in the game Timman-Schmidt, Indonesia 1983, from which its reputation has never recovered.

| 6 | dc | 02 | ♕a5 | 05 |
|---|----|----|----|----|
| 7 | ♖c1 | 04 | ♘e4 | 12 |

The old Fischer line. Later games (9, 11) indicated that 7 ... dc is more reliable.

| 8 | cd | 04 | ♘xc3 | 12 |
|---|----|----|----|----|
| 9 | ♕d2 | 04 | ♕xa2 | 12 |
| 10 | bc | 05 | | |

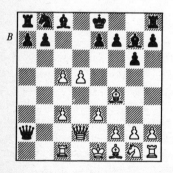

Here 10 ... ♕a5 is the main line, viz 11 ♗c4 ♘d7 12 ♘f3 0-0 13 ♗e5 ♗xe5 14 ♘xe5 f6 15 ♘f3 ♘xc5 16 ♕d4 ±. The famous 1971 Petrosian-

Fischer 2nd match game continued 12 ♘e2!? ♘e5 13 ♗a2 ♗f5? 14 ♗xe5 ♗xe5 15 ♘d4 ♕xc5 16 ♘xf5 and resulted in one of the great Armenian champion's most shattering victories.

Kasparov opts for something relatively new and unexplored.

| 10 | ... | | ♕xd2+!? | 14 |
|----|-----|----|----|----|
| 11 | ♔xd2 | 05 | ♘d7 | 15 |
| 12 | ♗b5 | 09 | 0-0 | 15 |
| 13 | ♗xd7 | 09 | ♗xd7 | 15 |
| 14 | e4 | 10 | | |

It is evident that Black will regain a pawn, but how will his position look afterwards? White's centre is suspiciously big and flexible, and indeed former Czech GM Ludek Pachman assessed this position as ±.

| 14 | ... | | f5 | 16 |
|----|-----|----|----|----|
| 15 | e5 | 11 | e6 | 19 |

A new move, obviously prepared by Kasparov, but Karpov did not seem perturbed by it. In fact, what occurs in this game is a rare instance of Kasparov's preparation being totally unsound. One other example is the celebrated gambit which Kasparov used to such effect in games 12 and 16 of their 1985 match. It is now said to be refuted by 1 e4 c5 2 ♘f3 e6 3 d4 cd 4 ♘xd4 ♘c6 5 ♘b5 d6 6 c4 ♘f6 7 ♘1c3 a6 8 ♘a3 d5 9 cd ed 10 ed ♘b4 11 ♗e2 ♗c5 (maybe 11 ... ♗d6!?) 12 ♗e3 ♗xe3 13 ♕a4+! (Karpov-Van der Wiel, Brussels (SWIFT)

1986. We would still like to see Kasparov's verdict on this and whether there are opportunities for resurrection.

Returning to the current game, 15 ... ♖fc8 is mentioned by Razuvayev in *Sovietsky Sport*, while 15 ... ♖ac8 16 c6 bc 17 d6 ed 18 ed ♖f6 (Schmidt-Gross, Naleczow 1984) still appears dubious after 16 c4! ♖xc5 17 ♗e3 ♖a5 18 f4 e6 19 d6 g5 20 ♘f3 gf 21 ♗xf4 (Dlugy). Perhaps 19 ... ♖a2+ and if 20 ♔c2 then 20 ... ♖a1. White may do better with 20 ♔d3 ♖xg2 21 ♘f3, sacrificing a pawn to keep Black's king's bishop out of the game for ever.

| 16 | c4 | *12* | ♖fc8 | *20* |
| 17 | c6! | *15* | | |

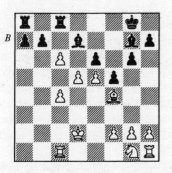

Thematic but attractive nonetheless. White ends up with a mighty passed pawn on d6 and a well protected pawn on e5 which stands firmly between Black's king's bishop and the sun.

| 17 | ... | | bc | *20* |

| 18 | d6 | *15* | c5? | *22* |

This may just lose, though it was played after only two minutes' thought and it must have been prepared. The best chance is 18 ... g5, though White stands better after 19 ♗xg5 ♗xe5 20 c5 ♖cb8 21 ♘f3 ♖b2+ 22 ♖c2! ♖b5 23 ♗f4 planning ♗e5.

| 19 | h4 | *20* | | |

To discourage ... g5 ideas in the future.

| 19 | ... | | h6 | *28* |
| 20 | ♘h3!! | *32* | | |

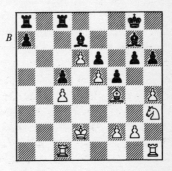

This beautiful move destroys Black's plans and leaves his game in positional ruins. Dlugy gives "!!" in the London bulletin, Razuvayev "!!" in *Sovietsky Sport*, while Kochiev and Osnos (Leningrad Tchigorin Club bulletin) ungenerously award only "!".

The point is that White wins if he can play his knight to d3 and bishop to e3. This manoeuvre fulfils a threefold purpose:

(i) it holds e5;

(ii) it keeps Black's king's bishop under lock and key;

(iii) it wins Black's pawn on c5.

In pre-game preparation Kasparov's team had only expected 20 ♘f3, when ... ♗c6 plus ... a5 is fine for Black. But by sacrificing several tempi and choosing a quite different route to d3 for his knight (h3-f2-d3, not f3-e1-d3), White simply blasts Black's whole conception. It was quite obvious from watching Kasparov's reaction that as soon as he saw ♘h3 he realized that he was losing – and in fact there was a markedly similar change of heart from his seconds in the press room.

| 20 | ... | | a5 | 32 |

There is nothing else left to do.

| 21 | f3 | 45 | a4 | 43 |
| 22 | ♖he1! | 80 | | |

Methodical, safety-first protection of the all-important e5 pawn. 22 ♘f2 is premature and allows turbulence after 22 ... g5.

| 22 | ... | | a3 | 55 |
| 23 | ♘f2 | 80 | a2 | 74 |
| 24 | ♘d3 | 81 | ♖a3 | 76 |
| 25 | ♖a1! | 91 | | |

No sense in ceding even a breath of freedom after 25 ♗e3 ♖xd3+ 26 ♔xd3 ♗xe5.

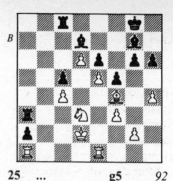

| 25 | ... | | g5 | 92 |

IM Ricardo Calvo (Spain) a denizen of the Park Lane analysis room, suggested as a last-ditch confusing tactic 25 ... ♖b8 26 ♖ec1 and now 26 ... g5 27 hg hg 28 ♗xg5 ♖8b3 29 ♘xc5 ♖b2+ 30 ♔e1 ♗xe5 31 ♘xd7 ♗xd6.

| 26 | hg | 104 | hg | 93 |
| 27 | ♗xg5 | 104 | ♔f7? | 121 |

Truly feeble, and generating groans of disappointment throughout the press room. He must still hazard 27 ... ♖b8, though after the clear-cut 28 ♔e2! ♗bb3 29 ♘xc5 ♖b2+ 30 ♔f1 (Razuvayev) White wins easily enough.

| 28 | ♗f4 | 113 | ♖b8 | 131 |
| 29 | ♖ec1 | 114 | ♗c6 | 141 |
| 30 | ♖c3 | 120 | ♖a5 | 142 |
| 31 | ♖c2 | 120 | ♖ba8 | 143 |
| 32 | ♘c1 | 121 | Resigns | |

Proof that, in spite of newfangled theories, protected passed pawns on d6 really are dangerous.

| Kasparov | ½ ½ ½ 1 0 | 2½ |
| Karpov | ½ ½ ½ 0 1 | 2½ |

# GAME SIX, 11 August

Spectators who had booked tickets for the delayed sixth game were treated to a lecture, cheese and wine, and a brilliant display of blitz chess. Korchnoi and Dlugy played a match of four 15-minute games on the stage which the audience were able to watch on the video-monitors move by move, with only a split-second time delay.

After the rest Kasparov played 1 e4 for the first time and Karpov countered with the super-solid Petroff Defence. Kasparov varied from the quickly drawn 15th game of their 1985 match and followed analysis which he himself had declared to be fine for Black in his recently published book of the match. But the analysis room broke into an uproar when Kasparov produced his 17th move improvement, which was only to be countered by Karpov's excellent 19th.

Kasparov put his head in his hands, thinking for a remarkable 69 minutes in an effort to press home a winning attack, but Karpov came out on top, and after the game had burned out to a rook and opposite bishop ending it was the Champion who was forced to play accurately to hold the draw.

### Kasparov-Karpov
*Petroff Defence*

**1   e4       00**

A rare guest in the first part of this match, possibly because the Petroff (used by Karpov) and the Scheveningen Sicilian (used by Kasparov) are such tough nuts to crack.

**1   ...           e5      03**
**2   ♘f3   00   ♘f6   04**

See page 27 for Karpov's Ruy Lopez loss to Sokolov at Bugojno. As Dlugy points out, "perhaps another reason for playing the Petroff".

| 3 | ♘xe5 | 02 | d6 | 05 |
|---|------|----|-----|----|
| 4 | ♘f3 | 04 | ♘xe4 | 05 |
| 5 | d4 | 04 | d5 | 12 |
| 6 | ♗d3 | 04 | ♘c6 | 18 |
| 7 | 0-0 | 05 | ♗g4 | 24 |
| 8 | c4 | 09 | ♘f6 | 24 |
| 9 | ♘c3 | 11 | ♗xf3 | 24 |
| 10 | ♕xf3 | 11 | ♘xd4 | 24 |
| 11 | ♕e3+ | 12 | | |

The first innovation over the board, though the queen check is known from Kasparov's own comments in his book of the 1985

55

world championship match. Game 15 had continued 11 ♖e1+ ♗e7 12 ♕d1 ♘e6 13 cd ♘xd5 14 ♗b5+ c6 and was drawn after a further eight moves. Ironically, Kasparov was later to say: "The first time that I felt that I might win the match was after the 15th game. It was the type of confidence which is sometimes lacking in contests between equals." (Quoted by Averbakh and Taimanov in their book of the match)

Both of us watched that game, but it is difficult to understand what it was that imbued Kasparov with so much confidence. Whatever it was, he certainly went straight on to score a crushing win with his controversial Sicilian Gambit in game 16.

There now follows a long forcing variation, probably foreseen by both players as far as White's 19th move, to judge by the respective clock usage.

| 11 | ... | | ♘e6 | 24 |
|----|-----|--|-----|----|

| 12 | cd | 12 | ♘xd5 | 25 |
|----|------|----|------|----|
| 13 | ♘xd5 | 12 | ♕xd5 | 25 |
| 14 | ♗e4 | 12 | ♕b5 | 32 |

Another paradox: "Black's position is solid and White is a pawn down." – Kasparov in his notes to game 15 in his book of the match! Actually, the further course of this game tends to reinforce that view.

| 15 | a4 | 13 |
|----|----|----|

"White forces the queen to the edge and hopes to utilise his lead in development to attack Black's king." (Dlugy)

| 15 | ... | | ♕a6 | 32 |
|----|-----|--|-----|----|
| 16 | ♖d1 | 13 | ♗e7 | 35 |

The natural consolidating move. If, more ambitiously, 16 ... ♗c5? Nunn gives the typically explosive 17 ♕f3 c6 18 ♖d7!! ♔xd7 19 ♕xf7+ ♗e7 20 ♗f5 with a terrible attack.

| 17 | b4 | 22 | 0-0 | 36 |
|----|----|----|-----|----|

No one would ever play 17 ... ♗xb4 against Kasparov, but various grandmasters were still able to amuse themselves conducting fantasy consequences in case of such foolhardiness:

Balashov (Leningrad bulletin): 18 ♗b2 0-0 19 ♕h3 g6 20 ♖d3 with the threat of ♕xh7+ and ♖h3-h8 mate.

Timman (press room): 18 ♕f3 c6 (18 ... ♘c5 19 ♖d4!) 19 ♖d7! 0-0 (19 ... ♔xd7 20 ♕xf7+ as above) 20 ♕h3 g6 21 ♗xg6 hg 22 ♗b2 ♘g7 23 ♕h6 etc.

White's b4 pawn here really is

56

poisoned.

**18 ♕h3** *28*

After 18 b5 ♖ad8! exploits the slight weakness of White's back rank to dislocate his attack.

White's development is excellent, but his rooks are still not connected, and in what is to come he suffers somewhat from absence of "luft".

**18 ... g6** *37*

**19 ♗b2** *29*

Again 19 b5 ♖ad8! is a complete answer. Tisdall advocated 19 ♕c3!? but Karpov pointed out to us the startling defence 19 ... ♘g5 20 ♗b2 ♗f6!! 21 ♕xf6 ♕xf6 22 ♗xf6 ♘xe4.

**19 ... ♕c4!** *59*

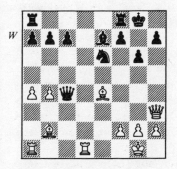

Found after immense cogitation. Dlugy calls it "an inspired defence, possibly overlooked by Kasparov".

Kasparov was patently thrown off course by this very fine queen interposition, a move which disrupts White's attack, threatens his king's bishop and queenside pawns and prevents sundry crude mating

tries on the other side of the board, e.g. 20 ♖d3? ♕xe4 21 ♕xh7+ ♔xh7 22 ♖h3+ ♗h4.

**20 ♖d7?!** *98*

69 minutes spent on this, and it is almost certainly not the best. An alternative, which leaves White's pieces less scattered, is 20 ♗d5 ♕c2 21 ♗e5 ♖ad8 22 ♖dc1 ♕d2 23 ♗xe6 fe 24 ♕xe6+ =. If 22 ♖d3 ♗g5! 23 ♖ad1 c6 24 ♕xe6 ♖xd5.

Balashov indicates here 20 ♗xb7 ♖ad8 21 ♖dc1 ♕f4 22 ♕c3 ♘d4 with counterchances.

**20 ... ♖ae8** *62*

Played *rapidamente*! Naturally not 20 ... ♕xe4? 21 ♕c3! f6 22 ♖xe7.

**21 ♗d5** *112*

The attack has fizzled out. What follows is spectacular but predictable.

**21 ... ♕xb4** *70*

**22 ♗c3** *114* **♘f4!** *90*

A neat riposte by Karpov, who is threatening ... ♕xc3 and ... ♘e2+ as well as ... ♘xh3+. The game now heads for a forced draw, though Black has some symbolic chances and plays on till adjournment.

| | | | | | |
|---|---|---|---|---|---|
| 23 | ♗xb4 | 114 | ♘xh3+ | 90 |
| 24 | gh | 114 | ♗xb4 | 91 |
| 25 | ♖xc7 | 114 | b6 | 103 |
| 26 | ♖xa7 | 116 | ♔g7 | 103 |
| 27 | ♖d7 | 125 | ♖d8 | 125 |
| 28 | ♖xd8 | 127 | ♖xd8 | 125 |
| 29 | ♖d1 | 128 | ♖d6 | 125 |
| 30 | ♖d3 | 130 | h5 | 126 |
| 31 | ♔f1 | 135 | ♖d7 | 129 |
| 32 | ♔g2 | 136 | ♗c5 | 132 |

Hereabouts Dutch GM Gennady Sosonko summed up the thoughts of many a professional player: "It's a draw of course, but in the US Open I would play on for ever."

| | | | | | |
|---|---|---|---|---|---|
| 33 | ♔f1 | 139 | h4 | 135 |
| 34 | ♗c4 | 141 | ♖e7 | 135 |
| 35 | ♖f3 | 141 | ♗d6 | 141 |
| 36 | ♔g2 | 142 | ♖c7 | 141 |
| 37 | ♗b3 | 143 | f5 | 145 |
| 38 | ♖d3 | 144 | ♗c5 | 145 |
| 39 | ♖c3 | 146 | ♔f6 | 145 |
| 40 | ♖c4 | 146 | g5 | 145 |
| 41 | ♖c2 | 151 | ♔e5 | 146 |

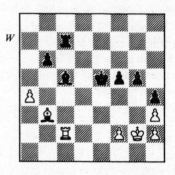

Kasparov now sealed **42 ♗c4**, but a **draw** was agreed without resumption.

| Kasparov | ½ ½ ½ 1 0 ½ | 3 |
|---|---|---|
| Karpov | ½ ½ ½ 0 1 ½ | 3 |

# GAME SEVEN, 13 August

In a dramatic time scramble Kasparov pulls off an amazing escape to turn the tables on Karpov and defend a losing position.

Karpov built up a crushing positional advantage from the opening, setting the scene for a vicious kingside attack, but experts were astounded when on move 25 he turned his attention to the queenside instead. Grandmasters looked at each other aghast, failing to understand why he had not continued to pile pressure on Kasparov's monarch at the critical moment. However, with both players increasingly short of time Karpov once again turned his attention to the kingside, and it was just when it appeared that he was winning again that Kasparov stunned observers with a brilliant 35th move to escape unhurt. In fact it became clear over the next few days that with the right follow-through Kasparov would have been the one left with winning chances.

After adjourning with a rook for a knight and two pawns Karpov offered the draw the following day, which Kasparov accepted without resuming.

Many grandmasters stressed that this game could prove a serious psychological blow to Karpov's chances, and Dlugy went further, adding that if Karpov were to lose the match then game 7 would be seen as one of the crucial turning points.

### Karpov-Kasparov
*Queen's Gambit Declined*

| 1 | **d4** | *00* | **d5** | *00* |
|---|--------|------|--------|------|

The Grünfeld is hauled into dry dock after its shipwreck in game 5.

| 2 | **c4** | *02* | **e6** | *00* |
|---|--------|------|--------|------|
| 3 | **♘c3** | *03* | **♗e7** | *01* |

Kasparov cannot have felt happy about this choice of opening. Of the nine games he has lost to Karpov no less than five have been as Black in Queen's Gambits.

| 4 | **cd** | *13* | **ed** | *01* |
|---|--------|------|--------|------|
| 5 | **♗f4** | *14* | **c6** | *04* |

Time for a brief history lesson involving three consecutive games from their 1985 match.

**Karpov-Kasparov**, game 20: 5 ... ♘f6 6 ♕c2 0-0 7 e3 c5 8 dc ♗xc5 9 ♘f3 ♘c6 10 ♗e2 ... ½-½ in 85.

**Kasparov-Karpov**, game 21: 5 ... c6 6 e3 ♗f5 7 g4 ♗e6 8 h4 ♘d7 9 h5 ♘h6 10 ♖c1 ... ½-½ in 44, but

White came close to winning.
**Karpov-Kasparov**, game 22: 5 ...
♘f6 6 e3 0-0 7 ♘f3 ♗f5 8 h3 c6 9
g4 ♗g6 10 ♘e5 ♘fd7 11 ♘xg6 fg
12 ♗g2 . . . 1-0 in 42. This was a
game of weird manoeuvres, in
many ways a forerunner of game 7
in London.

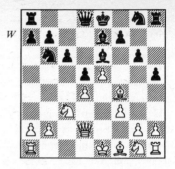

| 6 | ♕c2 | 16 | g6 | 06 |
| 7 | e3 | 17 | | |

7 0-0-0 ♘f6 8 f3 ♘a6 9 e4 ♗b4 is
Kochiev's suggestion if White
is aiming for a really sharp
struggle.

| 7 | ... | | ♗f5 | 07 |
| 8 | ♕d2! | 18 | | |

Much more dangerous than the
stereotyped developing move 8
♗d3, when 8 ... ♗xd3 9 ♕xd3
solves most of Black's problems
for him. 8 ♕d2 is a typically
Karpovian 'creeping' move which
leaves Kasparov with a serious
dilemma as to how to deploy his
queen's bishop in the remaining
course of the game.

| 8 | ... | | ♘d7 | 16 |
| 9 | f3 | 20 | ♘b6 | 18 |

We have noticed that Kasparov
likes to put the knight on b6 while
Karpov likes to have a pawn on b3
whenever this happens.

| 10 | e4 | 22 | ♗e6 | 18 |

10 ... de 11 fe ♗e6 12 ♘f3 looks
horrible for Black, mainly because
of the dark-square weaknesses
around his kingside.

| 11 | e5 | 25 | h5?! | 34 |

According to Nimzowitsch –
Black tries to blockade White's
mobile and dangerous kingside
pawns. The problem is that he can
never deploy his retarded king's
knight on a satisfactory square.
Dlugy recommends instead 11 ...
f5!?. This looks even uglier since it
cedes White a protected passed
pawn on e5 and hems in Black's
queen's bishop. Nevertheless, the
then World Junior Champion pro-
ceeds to justify it with a hard-to-
refute "concrete variation", as they
say in the USSR: 11 ... f5"!" 12 ♘h3
h6 13 ♗d3 ♕d7 14 ♗e3 g5 15 f4 g4
16 ♘f2 h5, sealing up the sensitive
kingside with a good position.
Nimzowitsch would have approved.

| 12 | ♗d3 | 34 | ♕d7 | 37 |
| 13 | b3 | 41 | ♗h4+ | 78 |

Trying to create a target for
future counterplay. 13 ... ♗f5 is
more natural, but somehow we
expected this check. What we did
not expect was that after Karpov's
obvious riposte . . .

**14 g3 55**

... Kasparov would ponder for a further seven minutes and then replace the bishop on e7, where it obstructs the path of his maimed king's knight.

**14 ... ♗e7 85**

It really looks more logical to play 14 ... ♗d8 followed by ... ♗c7 and ... 0-0-0. Now Black gets into a terrible tangle.

**15 ♔f2 60 ♗f5 97**
**16 ♗f1 71**

Karpov's handling of this obscure middlegame is unorthodox but very subtle. Here Black is cramped, therefore White just avoids any exchanges. This type of unexpected retreat also helps to nudge the opponent into worsening time trouble.

**16 ... ♔f8 113**

Kasparov too renounces the right to castle. It is beginning to look like Arabic chess from the 9th century A.D.

**17 ♔g2 77 a5 116**

In *Sovietsky Sport* Suetin proposes 17 ... ♔g7 18 h3 a5 19 g4 ♗e6 20 ♗d3 a4 21 ♘1e2 ab 22 ab ♖xa1 23 ♖xa1 hg 24 hg ♗xg4 with counterplay. We doubt, however, that Karpov would have proceeded so directly with the plan of g4. For example, 19 a3 comes into consideration, analogously to the game.

**18 a3 92 ♕d8 124**

Perhaps 18 ... ♔g7 is still pre-

ferable. The text permits White to bring out his king's knight.

**19 ♘h3 97 ♗xh3+ 130**

It is imperative to prevent ♘g5.

**20 ♔xh3 97 ♔g7 130**

20 ... g5 is wild and loosening, and Black would not have a shred of attack.

Philip Walden described White's king as "cocking a snook at the black forces".

| | | | |
|---|---|---|---|
| **21** | **♔g2** | **98 ♘d7** | **130** |
| **22** | **♗d3** | **101 ♘f8** | **130** |
| **23** | **♗e3** | **107 ♘e6** | **130** |
| **24** | **♘e2** | **117 ♘h6** | **134** |

The crunch has come. White can now win with 25 h3! followed by f4. In that case he can always crush ... h4 by Black with g4. Kasparov said to us: "After 25 h3! Black has no decent moves left." White can prepare a steamroller advance at his leisure with f4, ♖hf1 and f5. In contrast, Dlugy's 25 f4?! is premature, since Black plays 25 ... h4! at once, followed by ... ♘g4 with counterplay.

**25 b4?** *125*

This is a dreadful move, but the thought process behind it is clear: White is winning on the kingside already, where Black is more or less helpless. Therefore, seal up the queenside too, prevent Black's only counterplay (... c5) and Black can resign. In fact 25 h3 c5 26 f4! is a safe way to ignore ... c5, while 25 b4? simply creates a target for Black to seize on.

After this error Kasparov looked happy for the first time in the game. He swiftly passed through his time trouble, and Karpov himself even became short of time. Strangely, Soviet commentators such as Suetin and Kochiev did not even castigate 25 b4 with a "?", even though it is clearly the turning point of the game. Apropos Karpov's psychological approach to this position, some of Kasparov's comments about game 24 of their previous match are of interest: "Karpov plays à la Karpov! He does not hurry to force matters, but prefers consistently to strengthen his position." 25 b4? is an unfortunate way of so doing.

**25 ... ♕b6** *139*

**26 b5** *135*

Trying to repair the damage, but Black gets the chance to play the very move White has been desperately trying to prevent.

**26 ... c5** *139*

**27 ♘c3** *135*

And here 27 dc ♗xc5 28 ♗xc5 ♘xc5 29 ♘d4 is at least ±. In the final minutes of the session Karpov loses control.

**27 ... cd** *140*

**28 ♗xh6+** *135* **♖xh6** *140*

**29 ♘xd5** *135* **♕d8** *140*

**30 ♗e4** *135* **h4** *140*

Finally Black's curiously placed pieces start to make sense.

**31 ♖hf1** *140*

To meet ... h3+ with ♔h1.

**31 ... hg** *140*

**32 hg** *140* **♖c8** *144*

**33 ♖h1** *140*

Hoping to strike Black down along the h-file.

**33 ... ♖xh1?** *145*

And with five minutes on his clock Kasparov obliges. Correct is 33 ... ♗g5! 34 f4 ♖c5!! without exchanging yet on h1. In that case 35 fg ♖xh1 36 ♖xh1 ♖xd5 transposes to the game, but without allowing White a vital trick.

**34 ♖xh1** *141* **♗g5** *145*

**35 f4** *141* **♖c5!** *145*

62

Still a wonderful resource, and to judge by the six minutes taken over his reply, an out-and-out shock to Karpov.

White should now play 36 ♔g1!, when 36 ... ♖xd5 37 ♗xd5 ♕xd5 38 ♕h2 ♔f8 39 ♕h8+ ♔e7 40 fg leaves Black nothing better than resignation. The only reply to 36 ♔g1 is the resolute 36 ... f5!. The key line is now 37 fg fe 38 ♘f6 ♘f8 39 ♕f4 ♕e7 40 e6 ♕xe6 41 ♘e8+ ♔g8 42 ♖h8+ ♔xh8 43 ♕xf8+ ♕g8 44 ♕f6+ ♔h7 45 ♕e7+ ♔h8 46 ♕xe4 ♖c1+ 47 ♔g2 ♖c2+! with a draw, since alternatives to ♔g1 are too dangerous. But not 47 ... ♕a2+ 48 ♔h3, when White's king escapes up the h-file, while Black's remains mortally exposed. The position after 36 ♔g1! f5! is amazingly complex and fearfully risky for Black, but it is not yet proven that he is lost.

| 36 | fg? | 147 | ♖xd5 | 145 |
| 37 | ♗xd5 | 147 | ♕xd5+ | 145 |
| 38 | ♔h2 | 147 | ♕xe5 | 145 |
| 39 | ♖f1 | 147 | ♕xb5 | 149 |
| 40 | ♕f2 | 149 | ♘xg5?! | 149 |

Safety first with the clock flag hanging. After the superior 40 ... ♕d7! Black's queen and knight are a much fitter fighting force than White's queen and rook, and White would have to struggle to

draw.

| 41 | ♕xd4+ | 149 |

Kasparov now spent nine minutes sealing **41 ... ♔g8**, but again the **draw** was agreed without play being resumed. Black will have to make too many concessions to avoid perpetual check.

In this phase of the match (games 5, 6 and most of 7) we gained the impression that Kasparov had lost the initiative he established so clearly in games 1-4. The World Champion was frequently under pressure, and time and again he seemed puzzled by Karpov's moves. Then too, he often spent valuable minutes poring over moves which appeared to be forced. Karpov, on the other hand, was moving easily and swiftly and even looked better prepared for the openings than he had ever been before.

| Kasparov | ½ ½ ½ 1 0 ½ ½ | 3½ |
| Karpov | ½ ½ ½ 0 1 ½ ½ | 3½ |

63

# GAME EIGHT, 15 August

"It was tremendously tense. It was incredibly exciting, " Nigel Short exclaimed seconds after the game ended. "Karpov was in chronic time trouble and Kasparov decided he was going to win the game on time."

After surviving a blaze of complications Karpov emerged a pawn ahead but with only four minutes left for his last fourteen moves. Kasparov kept choosing the most complicated continuations available as the audience hovered on the edge of their seats and journalists were jam packed around the monitors, screaming their opinions of the position from either end of the press room. Match staffers began to shout out the times. "Mr Karpov has three minutes left." "After move 28 Mr Karpov has two minutes left." And finally, after move 29, "Mr Karpov has only one minute left." Josef Dorfman rushed into the commentary room and said in Russian that Karpov couldn't make the eleven moves needed "in such a position". As the final climactic moments were acted out Kasparov too appeared to become nervous – then suddenly Black's flag fell. The audience stood and applauded while a few members at the back called out "Gary". There was a short handshake and Karpov left the hall, followed almost immediately by the World Champion. As Kasparov exited from the back of the hotel he clenched his fist in a victory salute for the waiting photographers.

Back in the press room there had been some initial confusion as to whether Karpov had resigned or lost on time. As the facts became clearer and the excitement began to slowly ebb away, grandmasters exchanged opinions on the course of the game.

The opening had followed game 7 but with colours reversed. By move 16 Kasparov was beginning to build a dangerous attack against the Challenger's king. Kasparov sacrificed a pawn as his pieces poured into play, and Karpov was forced to cede the exchange. But Kasparov saw that taking the material would allow Karpov good drawing chances and after weighing up the odds the Champion refused to take the rook. His remarkable maxi-risk policy paid off handsomely as although Karpov emerged a pawn to the good he broke under the pressure.

So after one third of the match Kasparov was once again in the lead.

But that was not the main talking point. What was on everybody's mind was how Karpov had lost on time with so many moves to make.

American GM Nick de Firmian said: "The time scramble was so exciting I felt a knot in my stomach. The game was quite a mess but Kasparov's nerves were better in the complications." Michael Stean added the amusing observation that "if Kasparov continues to play like this they'll have to deduct betting tax from his winnings – he's a real gambler."

### Kasparov-Karpov
*Queen's Gambit Declined*

| 1 | d4 | *00* | d5 | *02* |

Up to now Karpov had never lost to Kasparov on the Black side of a Queen's Gambit Declined. As mentioned in game 7, Kasparov had lost five times after 1 d4 d5 – three times with the Orthodox Defence and twice in the Tarrasch.

| 2 | c4 | *00* | e6 | *03* |
| 3 | ♘c3 | *00* | ♗e7 | *03* |
| 4 | cd! | *05* | | |

It may seem strange to award this move an exclamation mark, but the trend of the more recent K-K games is beginning to show that 4 ♘f3 can grant White tedious pressure but only 4 cd can create genuine winning prospects. See, for example, game 22 of their last match or game 7 from London.

| 4 | ... | | ed | *03* |
| 5 | ♗f4 | *05* | ♘f6 | *13* |
| 6 | e3 | *06* | 0-0 | *17* |
| 7 | ♗d3 | *12* | c5 | *18* |

In game 22 of the previous match Karpov as White played 7 ♘f3 and

Black replied 7 ... ♗f5!? with approximate equality after 8 h3 c6 9 g4 ♗g6 10 ♘e5 ♘fd7 11 ♘xg6 fg.

| 8 | ♘f3 | *26* | ♘c6 | *21* |
| 9 | 0-0 | *28* | ♗g4 | *32* |

If 9 ... cd 10 ♘xd4 ♘xd4 11 ed and White has the edge after 11 ... ♕b6 12 ♖e1 ♗e6 13 ♘a4 ♕a5 14 a3 intending b4 and ♘c5. Or 11 ... ♗e6 12 ♘b5!? ♗g4 13 ♕b3 a6 14 ♘c3 ♕d7 15 ♗e5 ♗e6 16 ♘a4, again with a slight advantage.

| 10 | dc | *29* | ♗xc5 | *32* |

Avoiding the standard trap 10 ... d4? 11 ♘e4 ♘xe4 12 ♗xe4 ♗xc5 13 ♗xh7+ ♔xh7 14 ♕c2+ picking up the loose bishop on c5.

| 11 | h3 | *45* | | |

65

**11 ...        ♗xf3    40**

If 11 ... ♗h5 12 g4 ♗g6 13 ♗xg6 hg 14 ♗g5! is uncomfortable for Black. Also possible is the line suggested by de Firmian and Dlugy: 14 g5 ♘h5 15 ♕xd5 ♘xf4 16 ♕xc5 (not 16 ef since 16 ... ♗d6! equalises) 16 ... ♘xh3+ 17 ♔h2! ♕d7 18 ♔g3! f6 19 ♕c4+ ♖f7 20 gf gf 21 ♕g4! winning both a pawn and the game.

**12 ♕xf3    46    d4    40**
**13 ♘e4    46    ♗e7    63**

Black should try 13 ... ♘xe4 14 ♗xe4 de 15 ♕h5 f5 16 ♗xf5 ef+ 17 ♔h1 g6 18 ♗xg6 hg 19 ♕xg6+ ♔h8 and White may not have more than a draw. 15 fe may be more enduring. If 14 ♕xe4 then 14 ... g6 15 ed ♖e8 16 ♕f3 ♘xd4 17 ♕xb7 ♘e6 is fine for Black.

**14 ♖ad1    68**

Accumulating energy. Anyone who knows Kasparov's games would expect this.

**14 ...        ♕a5!?    93**
Played after almost half an hour's thought. The alternatives were 14 ... ♘d5 15 ♗h2, when Black's pieces are unstable, and 14 ... ♕b6. Not now 15 ♗d6 ♘d5! but 15 ♗g5! ♘d5 16 ♕h5 ♗xg5 17 ♘xg5 h6 18 ♗h7+ ♔h8 19 ♘xf7+ ♔xh7 20 ♕xd5 de 21 fe ♕xe3+ 22 ♔h1 Kasparov would be in his element in such a mêlée and it is no wonder that Karpov consumed so much time. In any case 14 ... ♕a5!? is a bold move which carries the fight to the opponent. White's queenside pawns are in danger of being massacred if he does not land a huge punch on the other wing.

**15 ♘g3    85**

Also critical was 15 ♗g5!, when Black must play 15 ... ♘d5 16 ♕h5 ♗xg5! 17 ♘xg5 h6 and perhaps he can defend.

**15 ...        de    99**
**16 fe    87**

Kasparov sacrifices a queenside pawn and receives in addition an isolated pawn on e3. In compensation he has freedom for all his pieces and two potent bishops. This is hard to evaluate since Black has no weak spots. In Moscow Botvinnik, Kasparov's mentor, was happy after this move. He felt White would soon have sufficient open lines for a decisive attack. In fact there is some resemblance, with White's open avenue of attack on the f-file, to a modernistic King's Gambit.

16 ...        ♕xa2    99

Not 16 ... g6? 17 ♗h6 and 18 ♘e4 with a winning attack.

17 ♘f5   91  ♕e6   104
18 ♗h6!  98

Initiating a decisive attack.

18 ...       ♘e8   107
19 ♕h5!!  104

A stroke overlooked by Karpov. White threatens 20 ♗xg7 and there is no good defence. If 19 ... ♘f6 20 ♘xe7+ ♘xe7 21 ♖xf6 gf (21 ... ♕xf6 22 ♗xh7+ and 23 ♗g5 wins) 22 ♗xf8 ♔xf8 (22 ... ♕xe3+ loses after 23 ♔h1 ♔xf8 24 ♗c4! ♘g6 25 ♕xh7 ♕e7 26 ♕h6+! – Tisdall) 23 ♕h6+ ♔e8 24 ♕g7!!. 19 ... gh loses to 20 ♘xh6+ ♔g7 21 ♘f5+ ♔h8 22 ♘xe7.

19 ...       g6   112
20 ♕g4  109  ♘e5  119
21 ♕g3  123

From this point until the end of the game Ray Keene stayed super-glued to his seat in the playing hall, transfixed by the excitement of the occasion. Adjacent was Professor Nathan Divinsky, chess star of the *Wogan* chat show and the resident Falstaffian wit of the BBC coverage. Kasparov radiated grim determination, while Karpov seemed more and more flustered. Occasionally he would reach out his hand to execute a move, and then retreat it suddenly.

The situation on the board is colossally interesting and double-edged. As in so many Kasparov games, his pieces are massed menacingly in front of the enemy king. But if he pauses to capture the exchange, his initiative may flicker and die. Karpov's position, meanwhile, is super-solid, and he does have an extra pawn. The struggle unfolding before us was not just one between two chessplayers, but two philosophies – Revolution and Reaction. Kasparov must try to storm through before Karpov can consolidate and emerge on top.

The universal verdict at the time amongst onlookers was that White should have tried 21 ♘xe7+ ♕xe7 22 ♗xf8 ♔xf8 23 ♕g3 ♘d6 24 ♗b1 followed by ♗a2, planning a doubling of rooks on the d-file. 23 ♕f4 is also possible. But Kasparov later refused to accept this view. He claimed that 21 ♕g3 was best and the exchange win variation virtually unwinnable. He had deliberately avoided this materialistic approach, counting instead on a much more devastating exploitation of Karpov's time trouble.

21 ...       ♗f6   136
22 ♗b5  133

An amazing move. Everyone expected 22 ♗xf8, though 22 ... ♔xf8 23 ♘d4 ♕b6 looks less promising than the other exchange win. 22 ♘d4 at once is possible, but Kasparov believed that with the text Black would be set insuperable practical problems and that White would always retain enough initiative for his pawn(s) to avoid losing.

| 22 | ... | ♘g7 | *141* |
| 23 | ♗xg7 | *135* | |

Timman pointed out that after 23 ♘d4 Black has the resource 23 ... ♕e7 24 ♖xf6 ♕xf6 25 ♖f1 ♘h5!, when he is better.

| 23 | ... | ♗xg7 | *141* |
| 24 | ♖d6 | *135* | ♕b3 | *141* |
| 25 | ♘xg7 | *136* | ♕xb5 | *142* |
| 26 | ♘f5 | *136* | | |

Not 26 ♘h5? ♘f3+! followed by ... ♕xh5, eliminating Black's most serious problem.

| 26 | ... | ♖ad8 | *146* |

It is natural enough to develop the rook when one has only four minutes left to reach move 40. Nevertheless, 26 ... f6! is accurate and holds after 27 ♘e7+ ♔g7 28 ♘f5+ ♔g8, but not 28 ... ♔h8? 29 ♘d4! ♕xb2 30 ♖dxf6 ♖xf6 31 ♕xe5 winning for White.

| 27 | ♖f6 | *140* |

Dlugy wrote: "White begins to play the most complicated moves, clearly planning to win on time."

| 27 | ... | ♖d2 | *147* |

27 ... ♖d7 is also hideously dangerous after 28 ♕g5 ♕b2 29 ♘h6+ followed by ♖6f2 or ♖6f4.

| 28 | ♕g5 | *142* | ♕xb2 | *148* |
| 29 | ♔h1 | *143* | | |

A horrible move to face in time trouble. Now ... ♖xg2 will not be check.

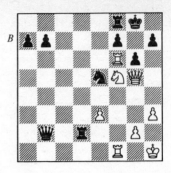

| 29 | ... | ♔h8 | *149* |

Panic, but what to do? In the bulletin Dlugy gives "29 ... ♖d7! 30 ♘h6+ ♔g7 31 ♖6f2 f6 32 ♖xf6 ♖xf6 33 ♖xf6 and White might draw." 31 ♖6f4 may be stronger, but White wins anyway in this line with 33 ♕xf6+! ♔h6 34 ♕f4+ ♔h5 35 g4+ ♔h4 36 ♖g1!.

| 30 | ♘d4 | *144* | ♖xd4 | *149* |
| 31 | ♕xe5 | *146* | | |

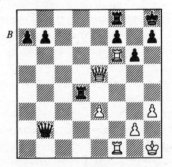

Black **lost on time**. To lose by time forfeit with ten moves still to play may be unique in the annals of the world championship. The position is still complicated and grandmasters argued for days about whether White was in fact winning. Sample variations are: 31 ... ♖d2 32 ♕e7 ♖dd8 33 ♖xf7 ♖xf7 34 ♖xf7 ♔g8! 35 ♖xh7 ♖f8 36 ♖h6 ♕g7 37 ♕e6+ ♕f7 38 ♖xg6+ ♔h7 39 ♖h6+ ♔g7 40 ♕d6 ♖d8! and

Black should survive. Better is 35 e4! g5 36 ♖f5 ♕d4 37 ♖xg5+ ♔h8 38 e5 winning.

After the game Karpov said that he could not understand what had happened to him in the time scramble and that his mind had felt "paralysed".

| | | | | | | | | | |
|---|---|---|---|---|---|---|---|---|---|
| Kasparov | ½ | ½ | ½ | 1 | 0 | ½ | ½ | 1 | 4½ |
| Karpov | ½ | ½ | ½ | 0 | 1 | ½ | ½ | 0 | 3½ |

# GAME NINE, 20 August

After the tragedy of game 7 and the disaster of game 8 Karpov wisely chose to take his first time out.

This time Jon Speelman was wheeled in to fight out a blitz match with Max Dlugy, who had beaten Korchnoi 2½-1½ in the earlier series. After four games Speelman and Dlugy were tied 2-2 and a five-minute "decider" also failed to provide a champion. So chief arbiter Lothar Schmid stepped in to stop the match and declare a draw, though Dlugy retained his blitz title.

After his break Karpov returned to the Park Lane for game 9 in a determined mood. Kasparov's surprise seventh move in the Grünfeld failed to unnerve him and he continued to play quickly and confidently. But at move 15 Kasparov produced an excellent move which stopped the Challenger dead in his tracks, and after 20 moves and less than three hours play Karpov had little choice but to accept the Champion's offer.

Experts saw the result as a further psychological boost for Kasparov, who had rehabilitated the Grünfeld with a vengeance.

One hour before play began Elaine Page, one of the stars of the musical *Chess*, led a quiet demonstration with members of the National Council for Soviet Jewry outside the match venue. As members of the group handed out leaflets, two members of the Soviet delegation, Alexander Fadeyev of *Pravda* and Vsevolad Kukushkin, distributed a short counter-statement to journalists accusing the demonstrators of trying to disturb the normal course of the competition.

Deputy press room chief Eric Schiller pointed out in turn that the demonstrators were nothing to do with the match or with the organisers.

**Karpov-Kasparov**
*Grünfeld Defence*

It seems that after a game in dry dock (game 7) the Grünfeld has been refitted and is ready for active service again.

| | | | | | | | | |
|---|---|---|---|---|---|---|---|---|
| 1 | d4 | 00 | ♘f6 | 00 | | | | |
| 2 | c4 | 00 | g6 | 00 | 4 | ♗f4 | 01 | ♗g7 | 01 |
| 3 | ♘c3 | 01 | d5 | 00 | 5 | e3 | 01 | c5 | 02 |

70

| 6 | dc | *01* | ♕a5 | *02* |
|---|-----|------|------|------|
| 7 | ♖c1 | *01* | dc | *03* |

Resolutely declining the disastrous adventures attendant on his 7 ... ♘e4 from game 5. The text is potentially boring, but has the inestimable advantage of being safer. Against Karpov this aspect is of vital significance. In *An Opening Repertoire for White* co-author Ray Keene wrote that after 7 ... dc Black has to seek "laborious equality", but in what follows Kasparov succeeds in removing some of the hard labour.

| 8 | ♗xc4 | *04* | 0-0 | *04* |
|---|------|------|------|------|
| 9 | ♘f3 | *04* | ♕xc5 | *05* |
| 10 | ♗b3 | *06* | | |

Dlugy speculates on the wild variation 10 ♘b5!? ♕b4+ 11 ♘d2 ♘e4 12 ♘c7 ♖d8 13 ♖c2 ♘xd2 14 ♖xd2 ♖xd2 15 ♕xd2 ♕xc4 or 14 ... ♗xb2 with ... ♗c3 to come. However, the sane 11 ... ♘a6 also looks playable.

| 10 | ... | | ♘c6 | *06* |
|---|-----|------|------|------|
| 11 | 0-0 | *08* | ♕a5! | *08* |

Black has previously come unstuck with 11 ... ♕h5, e.g. 12 h3 e5 13 ♗h2 ♖d8 14 ♘d2, Larsen-Tal from their Candidates match in 1965. On a5 Black's queen is quite safe – and influential.

| 12 | h3 | *09* | | |
|---|-----|------|------|------|

To hem in the black queen's bishop.

| 12 | ... | | ♗f5 | *17* |
|---|-----|------|------|------|
| 13 | ♘d4 | *10* | | |

Karpov was playing quickly and confidently and staring out into the audience, as he often does when he feels satisfied with his position. This argues that the former Champion was still contentedly following his own preparation. Kasparov, as the clock times show, was glued to the board, looking concerned and not particularly happy. All the more strange, therefore, that Black should now equalise so swiftly and efficiently. The old theory over which the text purports to improve was 13 ♕e2 ♘e4 14 ♘xe4 ♗xe4 15 ♘d2 ♗d5 16 ♗xd5 ♕xd5 = Hort-Uhlmann, Moscow 1971, or 14 ♘d5 e5 15 ♗h2 ♗e6 16 ♘c3 ♗xc3 17 bc ♖fe8 18 ♖fd1 ♖ad8 = Sanguinetti-Gheorghiu, Nice Olympiad 1974.

| 13 | ... | | ♗d7 | *26* |
|---|-----|------|------|------|

A self-possessed reply which keeps all of his options open.

| 14 | ♕e2 | *11* | | |
|---|-----|------|------|------|

Karpov continued to play quickly but if this is preparation it is, relatively speaking, not much better than Kasparov's in game 5. Black can probably play 14 ... ♘h5 15 ♘xc6 ♗xc6 16 ♗h2 ♖fd8 or 15 ♗h2 ♘xd4 16 ed ♗xd4 17 ♕xe7 ♗c6, or proceed as in the game. Perhaps Karpov had been awaiting the first line and still had something up his sleeve.

**14 ... ♘xd4 51**
**15 ed 11 e6! 51**

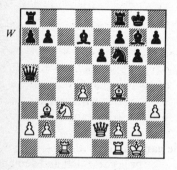

At first sight surprising, since it undermines his own dark squares, but look how the current time disparity (11-51) quickly evaporates. It had evidently been overlooked, or underestimated, by Karpov.

**16 ♗d2 38**

After this retreat it was obvious to everyone that White would settle for a draw, but 16 ♗e5, which appears to retain the initiative, is no good after Dlugy's line 16 ... ♗c6 17 ♕e3 ♖ac8 18 ♕f4 ♘d5

19 ♘xd5 ♗xd5 20 ♗c7 b6!. In such cases White's isolated queen's pawn can begin to tell as a significant static disadvantage.

**16 ... ♕b6 67**
**17 ♖fd1 39 ♗c6 69**

Of course not 17 ... ♕xd4?? 18 ♗g5!.

**18 ♗e3 65**

If 18 ♗g5 ♖ac8 and White is running out of ideas. If Black can complete his development he will stand better, so Karpov forces the issue.

**18 ... ♕a5 73**
**19 ♗d2 69 ♕b6 85**
**20 ♗e3 84 ♕a5 87**
**Draw Agreed**

Dlugy notes in the bulletin that "While this game may appear short and tedious, it was extremely important. Karpov will either need to demonstrate another way to play against the Grünfeld or refrain from playing 1 d4 altogether."

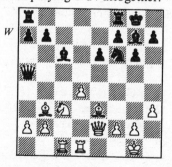

| | | | | | | | | | | |
|---|---|---|---|---|---|---|---|---|---|---|
| Kasparov | ½ | ½ | ½ | 1 | 0 | ½ | ½ | 1 | ½ | 5 |
| Karpov | ½ | ½ | ½ | 0 | 1 | ½ | ½ | 0 | ½ | 4 |

# GAME TEN, 22 August

Karpov comes right back into the match with a draw in the 10th game after producing an impressive theoretical novelty in a well analysed position. Despite the shock value of this innovation Kasparov replied after only fourteen minutes, obtaining two strong knights in the centre which forced Black to cede the bishop pair.

Karpov quickly exchanged off queens and a pair of rooks to go into an ending that looked drawish but where Black still had to defend accurately. After adjourning the players agreed to a draw, but a number of GMs criticised Kasparov for playing on too long after move 40 without sealing. Indeed, an hour after the end of play it became apparent that 43 a3 would have given the Champion dangerous zugzwang possibilities.

During the 9th game there had been so many chess fans unable to get tickets that BCF Congress Director Stewart Reuben had arranged for a large demonstration board to be set up in Green Park opposite the hotel, and had proceeded to comment on the game himself to the 150-strong overflow from the Park Lane. But with only three games left and demand for tickets outweighing their availability, the situation became more acute before the 10th. Remarking on the long queues that had formed in Piccadilly more than four hours before play, American games inventor Alex Randolph commented "It's getting like Harrods sale".

**Kasparov-Karpov**
*Queen's Gambit Declined*

| | | | | |
|---|---|---|---|---|
| 1 | d4 | 03 | d5 | 01 |
| 2 | c4 | 03 | e6 | 01 |
| 3 | ♘c3 | 03 | ♗e7 | 01 |
| 4 | ♘f3 | 04 | | |

4 cd has nearly always led to wild fighting games between the two. Towards the end of the London half Kasparov began to play more rationally.

| | | | | |
|---|---|---|---|---|
| 4 | ... | | ♘f6 | 01 |
| 5 | ♗g5 | 04 | h6 | 01 |
| 6 | ♗xf6 | 04 | ♗xf6 | 01 |
| 7 | e3 | 04 | 0-0 | 04 |
| 8 | ♖c1 | 05 | c6 | 07 |
| 9 | ♗d3 | 05 | ♘d7 | 12 |
| 10 | 0-0 | 05 | dc | 13 |
| 11 | ♗xc4 | 05 | e5 | 14 |
| 12 | h3 | 06 | ed | 14 |
| 13 | ed | 06 | | |

73

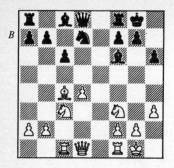

13 ... ♘b6 14 ♗b3 ♖e8 15 ♖e1
♗f5 16 ♖xe8+ ♕xe8 17 ♕d2 ♕d7
18 ♖e1 ♖d8 19 ♕f4 ± – Kasparov-
Karpov, match (23) 1985. Inciden-
tally, for those who remember
game 23, it is interesting to note
that FIDE President Florencio
Campomanes, in an interview with
*Sovietsky Sport*, selected it as his
favourite game of the 1985 match,
saying: "It was a grandiose draw
in which the conflict held everyone
in suspense from beginning to end,
in which both players demonstrated
models of play in attack and in
defence."

Instead of 18 ... ♖d8 in that game
Karpov himself recommended 18
... ♖e8!.

A subsequent example was 14 ...
♗f5 15 ♖e1 ♕d7 16 ♕d2 a5 17 a3
a4 18 ♗a2 ♖fe8 19 ♕f4 ♗e6 20
♗xe6 ♖xe6 21 ♖xe6 ♕xe6 22 ♕c7
♕b3 23 ♕xb7 ♕xb2 = Rashkovsky-
Belyavsky, Kiev (USSR Ch) 1986.
Perhaps 16 ♘e4!? is an improvement.

Karpov prefers to follow different
paths in order to eradicate the
central tension.

13 ... c5 14
14 ♗b3 20

An innovation. 14 ♘e4 was
tried in Tukmakov-Abramović,
Yugoslavia 1983, and Ionov-Goldin,
Minsk 1986. Both continued 14 ...
cd 15 ♘xf6+ ♗xf6 16 ♕b3, when
Abramović chose 16 ... ♕b6 17
♖fd1 ♗d7 18 ♖xd4 ♕xb3 19
♗xb3 ♖ac8, while Goldin played
16 ... ♘e4 17 ♖fd1 ♕f6 18 ♗d5
♘g5 19 ♘xd4. In neither case could
White boast a huge advantage.

14 ... cd 21
15 ♘d5 21 b6 43

Black could have played more
ambitiously with 15 ... d3, pro-
mulgated by IM Halifman in the
Leningrad special bulletin. He
continues with the opaque 16 ♕xd3
♗xb2 17 ♖ce1 ♘c5, or 17 ♖c2
♘e5. Karpov is not known to be
outstandingly fond of such adventures.

16 ♘xd4 43

Or 16 ♘xf6+ ♘xf6 17 ♕xd4
♗b7 18 ♕xd8 ♖axd8 19 ♘e5 ♗d5
20 ♘c6 ♗xc6 21 ♖xc6 ♖d7 22
♖fc1 ±.

16 ... ♗xd4 57

If 16 ... ♗b7 17 ♘c6 ♗xc6 18
♖xc6 ♗xb2 19 ♖d6!. Or 16 ... ♘c5
17 ♘xf6+ ♕xf6 18 ♗d5 ♗b7 19
♗xb7 ♘xb7 20 ♖c6! and White's
pieces dominate the centre.

| | | | | | |
|---|---|---|---|---|---|
| 17 | ♕xd4 | 43 | ♘c5 | 58 |
| 18 | ♗c4 | 44 | ♗b7 | 58 |
| 19 | ♖fd1 | 46 | ♖c8 | 65 |

**20  ♕g4  67**

With White's queen menacingly poised on g4 this position resembles game 16 from 1984 and game 11 from 1985, both situations with symmetrical pawn structures but where Kasparov's slightly more active and better centralised pieces enabled him to detonate whiplash attacks. Here Dlugy gives 20 ♖c3!? but 20 ... ♔h8! 21 ♖g3 ♘e6 holds.

**20  ...    ♗xd5  79**

If 20 ... ♖e8 21 b4. Obviously Karpov does not want to surrender bishop for knight in a wide open position, but at least the symmetrical pawn structure gives him good drawing chances.

**21  ♖xd5  80**

Writing in *Sovietsky Sport*, Suetin obscurely suggests 21 ♗xd5 ♕f6 22 ♖d4 ♖cd8 23 ♕d1. Maybe this is a misprint for 23 ♖cd1.

**21  ...    ♕e7  79**

**22  ♖cd1  88  ♕e4  92**

In the middlegame there is a great danger that White will launch a decisive attack based on b4 and ♖d7. In any case, trading queens pursues Karpov's general match strategy. Suetin suggests 22 ... ♖cd8 23 ♖xd8 ♖xd8 24 ♖xd8+ ♕xd8 25 b4 ♘b7 26 ♗xf7+ ♔xf7 27 ♕f3+ ♔g8 28 ♕xb7 ♕d2!.

| | | | | | |
|---|---|---|---|---|---|
| 23 | ♕xe4 | 107 | ♘xe4 | 92 |
| 24 | ♗a6 | 107 | ♘f6! | 92 |

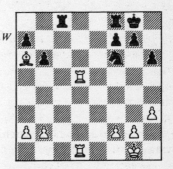

A useful tactic which prevents White from invading the 7th rank with his rook.

| | | | | | |
|---|---|---|---|---|---|
| 25 | ♗xc8 | 107 | ♘xd5 | 92 |
| 26 | ♗a6 | 107 | ♘f6 | 101 |
| 27 | f4 | 118 | | |

The position must be a draw, but White still has scope for manoeuvre. His kingside pawns are more mobile and the white bishop may dominate the black knight. If, however, 27 ♖c1 then 27 ... ♖d8! 28 ♗b5 ♘e8 =.

| | | | | | |
|---|---|---|---|---|---|
| 27 | ... | | ♖e8 | 104 |
| 28 | ♔f2 | 118 | ♔f8 | 110 |
| 29 | ♔f3 | 119 | ♖e7 | 115 |

75

| 30 | ♖d8+ | 127 | ♖e8 | 115 |
|----|-------|-----|------|-----|
| 31 | ♖xe8+ | 128 | ♘xe8 | 124 |
| 32 | ♔e4 | 130 | ♔e7 | 124 |
| 33 | ♗c4 | 134 | ♘c7 | 127 |
| 34 | ♔e5 | 137 | f6+ | 130 |
| 35 | ♔f5 | 138 | ♘e8 | 131 |
| 36 | ♔e4 | 138 | ♘c7 | 131 |

If 36 ... ♘d6+ 37 ♔d5 ♘xc4? 38 ♔xc4 a6 39 ♔d5 ♔d7 40 f5, or 38 ... ♔d6 39 ♔b5 ♔c7 40 ♔a6 ♔b8 41 f5 followed by b4 and a4-a5.

| 37 | h4 | 139 | ♔d6 | 133 |
|----|-----|-----|------|-----|
| 38 | ♔f5 | 140 | ♔e7 | 133 |
| 39 | ♔g6 | 143 | ♔f8 | 133 |
| 40 | ♔f5 | 144 | ♔e7 | 133 |
| 41 | ♔e4 | 151 | ♔d6 | 133 |
| 42 | g4 | 152 | | |

This move should have been sealed. We see here the same syndrome which deprived Kasparov of some chances in game 2. Botvinnik repeatedly stated that one should seal immediately one passes move 40, yet Kasparov constantly ignores this advice.

| 42 | ... | | ♔e7 | 135 |
|----|-----|-----|------|-----|
| 43 | b4? | 158 | | |

Still playing moves on the board. Now was the time to have a long think and then seal 43 a3!, which keeps up the tension while preventing a mass exchange of pawns on the queen's flank. White still has possibilities of winning in this case.

| 43 | ... | | ♔d6 | 136 |

After seven minutes' thought Kasparov now sealed **44 ♔f5** and the game was **drawn** without resumption.

GM Jon Speelman, a respected endgame authority and author of two works on the subject, thought at first that a zugzwang position could be forced by Kasparov from the adjournment,

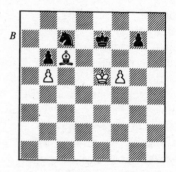

From the diagram Speelman demonstrated the variation 1 ... ♔f7 2 ♔d6 ♘xb5! 3 ♗xb5 ♔f6? 4 ♗d3, but missed the zwischenzug 3 ... g6! =. However, with a-pawns on the board (43 a3!) such ideas might have succeeded.

| Kasparov | ½ ½ ½ 1 0 ½ ½ 1 ½ ½ | 5½ |
|----------|---------------------|-----|
| Karpov | ½ ½ ½ 0 1 ½ ½ 0 ½ ½ | 4½ |

# GAME ELEVEN, 25 August

Despite the thrilling time scrambles of games 7 and 8, and the victories of 4 and 5, there was still no all-out favourite for the £10,000 Save and Prosper prize for the best game played in London – that is, until the 11th. And when the glittering display of chess fireworks had finally begun to fizzle out and the four and a half hours of unbroken tension resolved itself in a draw, the packed ballroom rose to their feet to give the two Soviet GMs a resounding ovation.

Karpov struck the first hammer-blow of the game with a prepared novelty in the Grünfeld which sent grandmasters reeling. The bombshell came with a brilliant exchange sacrifice (15 ♖xc6) which electrified the atmosphere throughout the hotel. Ten minutes later the initial reaction of the GMs gathered in the Mirror Room was that the innovation was almost winning for White. But Kasparov saw deeply into the complications, taking 38 minutes over his 16th move to find the only reply; and with his next, commentators began to re-evaluate the position. Karpov produced a clever zig-zag queen manoeuvre, and his knights also began to look extremely threatening, but the Champion countered with a pseudo-knight sacrifice of his own. Karpov entered into even wilder tactics, refusing to take refuge in a draw by perpetual check, but it eventually became apparent after Kasparov's 24th that Black stood no worse. After each move there were shouts and cheers from the excited grandmasters. Finally it was Kasparov who emerged from the smoke first, with a small but significant edge in an ending. But despite Kasparov's pressure and his own shortage of time Karpov defended very well to hold the draw with no difficulty.

Writing in the bulletin, IM Andrew Martin commented: "With games such as this it is still impossible to predict with any certainty who will win." But which pundit could best explain the majestic struggle we had witnessed? The task was left to Nathan Divinsky: "Today Kasparov out-Houdinied the great magician Karpov. He was chained with an opening surprise, handcuffed with a sequence of super-subtle queen moves, and then he broke out like Superman to almost win the game."

77

### Karpov-Kasparov
*Grünfeld Defence*

| | | | |
|---|---|---|---|
| 1 | d4 | 00 | ♘f6 | 00 |
| 2 | c4 | 00 | g6 | 00 |
| 3 | ♘c3 | 02 | d5 | 01 |
| 4 | ♗f4 | 02 | ♗g7 | 01 |
| 5 | e3 | 03 | c5 | 02 |
| 6 | dc | 03 | ♕a5 | 02 |
| 7 | ♖c1 | 03 | dc | 03 |
| 8 | ♗xc4 | 09 | 0-0 | 03 |
| 9 | ♘f3 | 11 | ♕xc5 | 03 |
| 10 | ♗b3 | 11 | ♘c6 | 04 |
| 11 | 0-0 | 11 | ♕a5 | 04 |
| 12 | h3 | 13 | ♗f5 | 04 |
| 13 | ♕e2 | 13 | | |

13 ♘d4 was game 9. When commenting on that we had no premonition of the bombshell that Karpov was to unleash in game 11.

| | | | |
|---|---|---|---|
| 13 | ... | | ♘e4 | 05 |
| 14 | ♘d5 | 14 | e5 | 11 |
| 15 | ♖xc6!? | 14 | | |

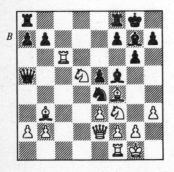

As soon as he played this startling exchange sacrifice Karpov turned to stare directly into the audience. This mannerism normally signifies

that he feels content with his position. When Karpov's gaze is glued to the board he is usually tackling a severe problem of some sort. Hit by the sacrifice, Kasparov looked as if the sky had fallen on his head, but he took a mere five minutes to reply. In fact, it seems Black could accept the Greek gift with relative impunity, viz 15 ... bc 16 ♘e7+ ♔h8 17 ♘xc6 ♕b6 18 ♘cxe5 ♗e6! 19 ♘c4 ♗xc4 20 ♕xc4 ♘c5. Of course acceptance is dangerous, but it should not lose.

| | | | |
|---|---|---|---|
| 15 | ... | | ef | 16 |
| 16 | ♖c7 | 15 | | |

Double-edged, but clearly part of Karpov's preparation. The rook is aggressive here, but also exposed.

| | | | |
|---|---|---|---|
| 16 | ... | | ♗e6 | 53 |

The clock times indicate that Black, at least, had exhausted his pre-game analytical homework.

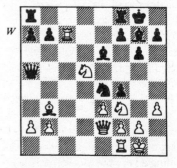

This game is full of amazing tactical resources, and Black's last move obliges White to tread carefully himself. If he does not, he could fall for 17 ♖xb7 ♗xd5 18 ♖b5 ♘c3!! 19 bc ♗xf3 20 gf ♕xc3, or 17 ♘e7+ ♔h8 18 ♖xb7 ♘d6! 19 ♘c6 ♕c5 20 ♖c7 ♕b6. In the first line Kochiev (Leningrad bulletin) also mentions 17 ... ♘d6, while in the second Suetin in *Sovietsky Sport* suggests 18 ♖fc1.

**17 ♕e1 19 ♕b5! 58**

And now it was Karpov's turn to think. Exchanging on e1 would of course leave White will all he desires – a queen exchange plus dominating pieces in a simplified position.

**18 ♘e7+ 46 ♔h8 59**

White's forces exude aggression but there is some danger that those on the seventh rank may become stranded.

**19 ♗xe6 46**

White seems to be doing all the forcing, but Dlugy in the London bulletin shows that Black has plenty of shots available to him as well: 19 ef? ♘g3! 20 fg ♕b6+, or 19 ♘d4 ♕e5 20 ♘xe6 fe 21 ♖xb7 f3 22 g3 ♘xg3 23 fg f2+ 24 ♖xf2 ♕xg3+ 25 ♔f1 ♖xf2+ 26 ♕xf2 ♖f8.

**19 ... fe6 66**

**20 ♕b1! 51**

Sliding along the back rank, Karpov nevertheless succeeds in aiming a very big long-range punch indeed at g6. Incredibly Black's resources, in spite of the ragged nature of his structure, easily hold up.

**20 ... ♘g5! 78**

Simultaneous defence and attack.

**21 ♘h4 79**

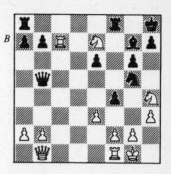

White is powering up for a sac' on g6.

21 ♘xg5 is feeble, viz 21 ... ♕xg5 22 ef ♖xf4 23 ♖xb7 ♖af8 with tremendous counterplay.

**21 ... ♘xh3+ 90**

Playing for a win by "luring Karpov into wild tactics" (Dlugy). Suetin (*Sovietsky Sport*) demonstrates an immediate draw with 21 ... fe 22 ♘exg6+ hg 23 ♘xg6+ and perpetual check. If 21 ... fe 22 fe? ♘xh3+ 23 gh ♕g5+ 24 ♘g2 ♗e5 with a devastating counterattack.

**22 ♔h2 79**

Not 22 gh ♕g5+ 23 ♘g2 f3.

**22 ... ♕h5 95**

**23 ♘exg6+ 83**

Alternatives:

a) **23 ♔xh3 g5** is out of the question for White.

b) **23 ♘hxg6+ hg 24 ♕xg6 ♕h7** (24 ... ♕e5 25 ♔xh3 ♖f6 26 ♔g4!!

threatening ♖h1+) 25 ♕xh7+ ♔xh7 26 ♔xh3 fe 27 ♔g4 ♖f7 =.

| 23 | ... | hg | 95 |
| 24 | ♕xg6!? | | 86 |

Incredibly brave, still striving for a win (which is not there). Evidently 24 ♘xg6+ ♔g8 25 ♘e7+ leads to perpetual check.

| 24 | ... | ♕e5! | 98 |

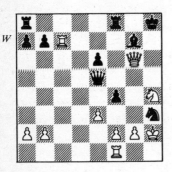

Played nonchalantly by Kasparov – and quickly too. Karpov now pondered for 41 minutes, which means he either overlooked 24 ... ♕e5 (expecting only 24 ... ♕h7) or underestimated the move. There is now a morass of complications:

a) **25 ♖xb7** fe+ 26 ♔xh3 ♖xf2 27 ♖h1 is given by Dlugy, who says that White's attack has stopped but does not explain why. Meanwhile Suetin gives 25 ... ♘xf2 26 ♘f3 ♕f6 27 ♕h5+ ♕h6 28 ♕xh6+ ♗xh6 29 ♖xf2 fe 30 ♖c2 ♖ac8. This looks more convincing on the whole.

b) **25 ♕c2** fe+ 26 ♔xh3 ♔g8 27 f4 e2 28 fe ef♕ 29 ♖xg7+ ♔xg7 30 ♕g6+ =.

c) **25 ♖xg7** ♕xg7 26 ♕h5+ ♔g8 27 gh fe 28 ♖g1 ef 29 ♖xg7+ ♔xg7 leads to a draw. However, the interposition of 25 ... fe+! causes White grave problems, e.g. 26 f4 ♕xg7 27 ♕h5+ ♔g8 28 gh ♕xb2+ 29 ♔h1 ♖f7, or 26 ♕g3 ♕xg7 27 ♘g6+ ♔g8 28 ♘xf8 ♘g5!! 29 ♘d7 ♖d8 30 ♘e5 e2 31 ♖e1 ♖d1 32 ♘d3 ♕h7+ 33 ♔g1 ♕xd3 34 ♕xg5+ ♔f7 and Black will eventually win. This interesting analysis stems from Dlugy's comments in the London bulletin.

| 25 | ♖f7!? | | 127 |

In a way the least expected move of all. Events now proceed like clockwork into an ending where Black has a minimal advantage.

| 25 | ... | ♖xf7 | 111 |
| 26 | ♕xf7 | 127 | ♘g5 | 111 |
| 27 | ♘g6+ | 127 | ♔h7 | 111 |
| 28 | ♘xe5 | 127 | ♘xf7 | 112 |
| 29 | ♘xf7+ | 127 | ♔g6 | 112 |
| 30 | ♘d6 | 127 | fe | 113 |
| 31 | ♘c4! | 128 | | |

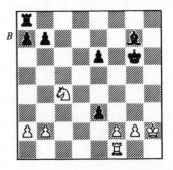

Without this White would be in real trouble.

| 31 | ... | | ef | *119* |
|----|-----|------|------|-------|

Perhaps 31 ... b5 32 ♘xe3 ♗xb2 33 ♖b1 ♗e5+ 34 g3 a6, though it is very little.

| 32 | ♖xf2 | *128* | b5 | *121* |
|----|------|-------|------|-------|
| 33 | ♘e3 | *128* | a5 | *122* |
| 34 | ♔g3 | *136* | a4 | *124* |
| 35 | ♖c2 | *139* | ♖f8 | *125* |
| 36 | ♔g4 | *144* | ♗d4 | *132* |
| 37 | ♖e2 | *146* | ♗xe3 | *141* |
| 38 | ♖xe3 | *146* | ♖f2 | *141* |
| 39 | b3 | *147* | ♖xg2+ | *146* |
| 40 | ♔f3 | *147* | ♖xa2 | *146* |
| 41 | ba | *147* | | |

and the players agreed to a **draw**.

A fitting conclusion to a grand struggle and a worthy winner of the Save and Prosper prize. This prize was judged by a panel of English GMs (Miles, Speelman, Mestel, Short, Chandler) and Bill Hartston. At the suggestion of co-author and Organising Committee Chairman Ray Keene the prize (split £5,000 to each player) was awarded in the form of British gold sovereigns from the reign of Queen Victoria. These were provided by match medallists B.A.Seaby. Perhaps this will set a trend for prize money in UK grandmaster tournaments – a return to the Gold Standard.

| **Kasparov** | ½ ½ ½ 1 0 ½ ½ 1 ½ ½ ½ | **6** |
|--------------|------------------------|-------|
| **Karpov** | ½ ½ ½ 0 1 ½ ½ 0 ½ ½ ½ | **5** |

# GAME TWELVE, 27 August

After the unrelenting tension of game 11, the 12th and final game in London was a quiet affair. Karpov revealed yet another opening innovation – again with the move ... c5. Kasparov played actively in the centre but was careful to keep the draw in hand, steering away from any unclear positions. After a series of exchanges this uninspiring struggle was agreed drawn in an ending where White could make no tangible progress. As the last game in London, and therefore the last that almost all spectators and experts would see live, just about everyone had hoped for a hard fought and nail-biting final struggle. But Kasparov cannot be blamed for ensuring that he always had the draw in hand, while Karpov's opening novelty appears to have been a great success.

**Kasparov-Karpov**
*Queen's Gambit Declined*

| | | | | |
|---|---|---|---|---|
| 1 | d4 | 00 | | |

It is interesting to examine a few statistics concerning the openings of Kasparov's games with Karpov over their three matches. The halfway stage affords a convenient opportunity for this, and for considering what might occur in the second half of this tale of two cities.

Since game 28 of their first match neither player has opted for anything other than 1 d4 or 1 e4! This could well be a pointer to the future, and of the twelve games so far in this match, eleven have opened with d4 and only one with e4.

| | | | | |
|---|---|---|---|---|
| 1 | ... | | d5 | 00 |

In their world title matches there have now been five games with Kasparov's 1 d4 being met by 1 ... d5. The score after the present game is one win to Kasparov (game 8), no losses, four draws.

| | | | | |
|---|---|---|---|---|
| 2 | c4 | 00 | e6 | 00 |
| 3 | ♘c3 | 00 | ♗e7 | 00 |
| 4 | ♘f3 | 01 | ♘f6 | 00 |
| 5 | ♗g5 | 01 | h6 | 01 |
| 6 | ♗xf6 | 02 | ♗xf6 | 01 |
| 7 | e3 | 02 | 0-0 | 01 |
| 8 | ♖c1 | 02 | | |

It is revealing to see what Kasparov himself has to say about this variation: "A slight (even the most minimal) openings advantage to White, guaranteeing a draw, but ensuring the initiative and the possibility, should the opportunity offer itself, of playing for a win." In any case, with respect to the present game it is our view that, before the transfer from the banks of the Thames to the banks of the Neva, Kasparov had decided to limit his expenditure of energy and stay one point ahead.

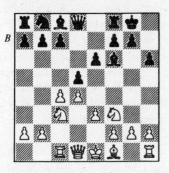

| 8 | ... | | c6 | 10 |
| 9 | ♗d3 | 02 | ♘d7 | 11 |
| 10 | 0-0 | 03 | dc | 13 |
| 11 | ♗xc4 | 03 | c5 | 16 |

Karpov varies first from game 10, but judging from the clock times Kasparov was not particularly shocked.

| 12 | ♕e2 | 05 | a6 | 17 |
| 13 | ♖fd1 | 08 | cd | 18 |

Dlugy gives 13 ... b5? 14 ♗b3 cd 15 ♘xd4 ♗b7 16 ♘xe6!. Another reason for avoiding 13 ... b5? is 14 dc bc 15 c6, when Black's pawn structure starts to sag.

**14 ♘xd4 21**

14 ed is tempting, but possibly not in Kasparov's game plan. Centralising his pieces cannot be bad,

and Black must still struggle to equalise.

**14 ... ♕e7! 19**

Once again 14 ... b5 15 ♗b3 ♗b7 16 ♘xe6! is a quick way to vanish down the London sewers. Karpov is much too alert to fall for that sort of thing.

**15 ♘e4 23**

Inaugurating a prelate-pursuit.

| 15 | ... | | ♗e5 | 20 |
| 16 | ♘f3 | 29 | | |

Driving the black bishop into a priest hole on b8. Another idea, though possibly unacceptably aggressive for the present occasion, was Suetin's 16 f4 ♗b8 17 ♗d3, or 17 ♕h5 ♘f6 18 ♕h4 ♘d5 19 ♕g3.

| 16 | ... | | ♗b8 | 23 |
| 17 | ♕d2 | 37 | | |

White utilises his superior coordination to plan a cavalry invasion on d6. The whole theme of White's play is to force an exchange of his queen's knight for Black's king's bishop and then dominate the c- and d-files with his well-developed pieces.

| 17 | ... | | b5 | 49 |
| 18 | ♗e2 | 42 | | |

Or 18 ♗b3 ♗b7! 19 ♕xd7 ♕xd7 20 ♘f6+ gf 21 ♖xd7 ♖a7 22 ♘d4 ♗a8! = – a variation given by Norwegian GM Simen Agdestein, who was in London for the Lloyds Bank Masters (won by him with 8/9).

| 18 | ... | | ♘f6 | 61 |

83

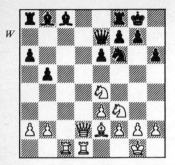

18 ... ♗b7 reveals the point of 18 ♗e2, i.e. the possibility of transferring the bishop to the h1-a8 diagonal before Black can disentangle his forces: 18 ... ♗b7 19 ♕xd7 ♕xd7 20 ♖xd7 ♗xe4 21 ♘d2 ♗g6 22 ♗f3 ♖a7 23 ♖xa7 ♗xa7 24 ♖c6, or 21 ... ♗d5 22 ♗f3 ♗xf3 23 ♘xf3 when, as Dlugy puts it, "White, in possession of the two open files, is winning".

**19 ♘xf6+ 82**

This extinguishes the fire of the position and leaves Karpov with only symbolic difficulties, which he solves handily. Dlugy and Suetin (the latter the sole Soviet GM correspondent present in London) were both for the more adventurous 19 ♘c5! ♖a7 20 ♘d4 ♖c7 21 ♘db3 or 21 b4 ±. Not, though, 19 ♘d6 ♗xd6 20 ♕xd6 ♕xd6 21 ♖xd6 ♗b7 = (22 ♖c7 ♘e8!).

**19 ... ♕xf6 62**
**20 ♕d4 82**

This time Kasparov, sitting on his point lead, goes for the swap.

| | | | | |
|---|---|---|---|---|
| **20** | **...** | | **♗b7** | **92** |
| **21** | **♕xf6** | **90** | **gf** | **92** |
| **22** | **b3** | **95** | | |

Or 22 ♖d7 ♗d5 and ... ♖a7 (B.Vladimirov, Leningrad bulletin).

| | | | | |
|---|---|---|---|---|
| **22** | **...** | | **f5** | **94** |
| **23** | **g3** | **97** | **♗xf3!** | **99** |

No nonsense. The position is now dead level.

| | | | | |
|---|---|---|---|---|
| **24** | **♗xf3** | **98** | **♖a7** | **99** |
| **25** | **♖c6** | **100** | **♔g7** | **108** |
| **26** | **♗e2** | **119** | **♗e5** | **108** |
| **27** | **h3** | **122** | **♗f6** | **112** |
| **28** | **♖dd6** | **125** | **♖fa8** | **112** |
| **29** | **♔g2** | **128** | **♗e7** | **119** |
| **30** | **♖d2** | **128** | **b4** | **122** |
| **31** | **g4** | **130** | **fg** | **123** |
| **32** | **hg** | **130** | **a5** | **123** |
| **33** | **f4** | **135** | **♖d8** | **123** |
| **34** | **♖xd8** | **136** | **Draw Agreed** | |

This game concluded the historic London leg.

The closing ceremony, hosted by Save and Prosper in the ballroom of the Park Lane Hotel, took place on Saturday 30 August.

Former Prime Minister James Callaghan was the guest of honour. He proved to be a spontaneous and witty speaker, rousing his audience with a humorous speech and amusing them with his quick responses.

| | | | |
|---|---|---|---|
| Kasparov | ½ ½ ½ 1 0 ½ ½ 1 ½ ½ ½ ½ | 6½ |
| Karpov | ½ ½ ½ 0 1 ½ ½ 0 ½ ½ ½ ½ | 5½ |

# LENINGRAD

## GAME THIRTEEN, 5 September

Here in Neva Neva Land the level of chess culture is remarkable. It is possible to sit down to your breakfast of blintzes and find detailed comments by grandmasters on the previous night's K-K game in your morning copy of *Pravda* or *Sovietsky Sport*.

The venue, the concert hall of the Hotel Leningrad, is decked out beautifully in red with a white silk backdrop which features only the match logo. This half of the match does not, of course, have any private sponsors.

Just before play was due to begin, the mayor of Leningrad, Vladimir Khodirev, welcomed the players to his city, while in the background the players exchanged a few words.

One big contrast was immediately apparent. The protagonists had put away their flashy white and light blue suits from London. Instead they were attired most conservatively, Karpov in a grey suit with red tie and Kasparov in a dark beige suit.

In the game Kasparov appeared to be under heavy pressure, but after Karpov lost his way in the mutual time scramble it eventually became clear that Kasparov had missed a dangerous continuation at move 33.

The opening, a Grünfeld Defence, duplicated the variation of game 3 from London. Karpov produced a novelty on move 10, thrusting his f-pawn forward instead of retreating his advanced knight. The middle-game soon developed into a kind of blocked trench warfare which finally opened up in the time scramble —only to peter out to a draw.

Meanwhile, down in the press room Vitaly Sevastianov, former cosmonaut and now President of the USSR Chess Federation, made a short statement and then answered questions from the press – the first of a series of press conferences, reflecting a slightly more open attitude from the match organisers. Sevastianov began by praising the match organisers in London. He added: "We hope the second half of the contest conducted in Leningrad will be as creative, more interesting as regards the sporting qualities and organised as well as the one carried out in London."

### Karpov-Kasparov
*Grünfeld Defence*

| 1 | d4 | 00 | ♘f6 | 00 |
|---|-----|-----|------|-----|
| 2 | c4 | 00 | g6 | 00 |
| 3 | ♘f3 | 04 | ♗g7 | 01 |
| 4 | g3 | 06 | | |

Karpov reverts to the treatment used in game 3. Evidently he has not yet found a revival of his idea from game 11.

| 4 | ... | | c6 | 05 |
|---|-----|-----|------|-----|
| 5 | ♗g2 | 06 | d5 | 05 |
| 6 | cd | 06 | cd | 05 |
| 7 | ♘c3 | 06 | 0-0 | 06 |
| 8 | ♘e5 | 06 | e6 | 06 |
| 9 | 0-0 | 07 | ♘fd7 | 07 |
| 10 | f4 | 07 | | |

| 10 | ... | | f6 | 07 |
|---|-----|-----|------|-----|

Not new, but unusual. Boleslavsky once suggested 10 ... ♘xe5 11 fe f6 as the correct antidote, but Kasparov prefers a more recondite line.

| 11 | ♘f3 | 12 | ♘c6 | 10 |
|---|-----|-----|------|-----|
| 12 | ♗e3 | 17 | | |

12 e4 is worth a thought.

| 12 | ... | | ♘b6 | 17 |
|---|-----|-----|------|-----|

Once again Kasparov steers a knight to b6 and Karpov reacts with b3. If 12 ... f5 13 ♘e5 ♘f6 14 ♘xc6 bc and White stands structurally better. Kasparov plans to bring his knight to e4 without creating pawn weaknesses.

| 13 | ♗f2 | 22 | f5 | 30 |
|---|-----|-----|------|-----|
| 14 | ♘e5 | 22 | ♗d7 | 30 |
| 15 | ♕d2 | 36 | ♘c8 | 55 |
| 16 | ♕e3 | 48 | | |

An original looking move. If now 16 ... ♘d6? 17 ♘xc6 ♗xc6 loses the c6 pawn with check.

| 16 | ... | | ♔h8 | 58 |
|---|-----|-----|------|-----|
| 17 | ♖fd1 | 50 | | |

Not now 17 ♘xc6 ♗xc6 18 ♕xe6?? ♖e8 19 ♕f7 ♘d6 nailing White's queen. A double-edged alternative is 17 g4 ♘xe5 18 de fg 19 ♕g3 h5 20 h3 g5 (Gufeld in *Sovietsky Sport*).

| 17 | ... | | ♘d6 | 60 |
|---|-----|-----|------|-----|
| 18 | b3 | 63 | ♖c8 | 82 |

If 18 ... ♕e7 19 ♖ac1 ♖fc8 20 ♘xd5 ed 21 ♖xc6 followed by ♘xg6+ wins. This variation demonstrates that White is really exerting serious pressure, in spite of the blocked nature of the position.

| 19 | ♖ac1 | 66 | ♗e8 | 89 |
|---|-----|-----|------|-----|
| 20 | ♗e1 | 72 | ♗f6 | 92 |
| 21 | ♘a4 | 83 | b6 | 101 |
| 22 | ♘b2 | 87 | ♘e4 | 107 |
| 23 | ♘bd3 | 92 | g5 | 110 |

Black has to do something, and Kasparov now makes an excellent job of confusing the issue as the fifth hour of play approaches.

| | | | |
|---|---|---|---|
| 24 | ♘xc6 | 99 | ♗xc6 | 115 |
| 25 | ♘e5 | 118 | gf | 117 |
| 26 | gf | 118 | ♗e8 | 129 |
| 27 | ♕h3 | 130 | ♖g8 | 132 |
| 28 | ♔f1 | 131 | ♖xc1 | 136 |
| 29 | ♖xc1 | 131 | h5!? | 138 |

The press centre went into shock. Surely Black must lose now that his king's position is full of gaping self-inflicted wounds. But the bishop on e8 is a stalwart defender of h5, and if Black shrinks from this bold measure ♕h6 will be strong.

**30 ♗b4? 137**

As time pressure approaches Karpov wavers. Correct is Gufeld's 30 ♗f3 ♕e7 31 ♖c8 ♕g7 32 ♗g2 with continuing heavy pressure.

**30 ... a5 140**

**31 ♗a3? 139**

And here the bishop has to return to e1. Both players were now looking exceptionally nervous. And suddenly, having been squeezed for so long, Kasparov whips up a counterattack in the dying minutes of the session.

| | | | |
|---|---|---|---|
| 31 | ... | | ♗xe5 | 141 |
| 32 | de | 141 | ♖g4 | 143 |
| 33 | ♗xe4 | 145 | | |

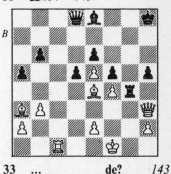

| | | | |
|---|---|---|---|
| 33 | ... | de? | 143 |

And here Black even misses a winning chance: 33 ... fe 34 e3 d4 35 ♗d6 ♕a8; or 34 ♔e1 d4 35 ♗d6 e3; or 34 ♕e3 ♕h4 35 ♖c8 ♖xf4+ 36 ♔g2 ♕g4+; or 34 ♗d6 d4 35 ♖c7 ♗g6 36 ♖e7 ♕a8 37 ♖xe6 ♕c6. White's problem in all these lines is his queen stuck on h3.

| | | | |
|---|---|---|---|
| 34 | ♗d6 | 145 | ♖xf4+ | 143 |
| 35 | ♔e1 | 145 | ♖g4 | 143 |
| 36 | ♕e3 | 145 | ♕g5 | 143 |

The final moves were banged out, but the draw is now clear.

| | | | |
|---|---|---|---|
| 37 | ♕xg5 | 148 | ♖xg5 | 146 |
| 38 | ♖c8 | 148 | ♖g8 | 146 |
| 39 | e3 | 149 | h4 | 147 |
| 40 | h3 | 149 | a4 | 148 |

**Draw Agreed**

| | | | | | | | | | | | | | | | | |
|---|---|---|---|---|---|---|---|---|---|---|---|---|---|---|---|---|
| Kasparov | ½ | ½ | ½ | 1 | 0 | ½ | ½ | 1 | ½ | ½ | ½ | ½ | ½ | | 7 |
| Karpov | ½ | ½ | ½ | 0 | 1 | ½ | ½ | 0 | ½ | ½ | ½ | ½ | ½ | | 6 |

# GAME FOURTEEN, 8 September

With the most profound strategic achievement of the match so far Kasparov scored a tremendous victory to take an 8-6 lead. After some super-subtle rook manoeuvres which left onlookers baffled, the World Champion gained a winning advantage by penetrating with a knight to c5, totally disrupting the black forces. As Kasparov confidently wandered about the stage the video cameras showed a poignant close-up of Karpov, urgently seeking a solution to his problems.

After a mutual time scramble Kasparov adjourned in an ending on the point of winning a pawn. Reached by telephone, Yuri "Mr Endgames" Averbakh pronounced Black as "helpless", and it came as little surprise the next day when Karpov resigned without resuming.

The opening was the first Ruy Lopez of the match. Both players followed home preparation for 20 moves before Kasparov decided to reject a pawn offer and turn his attention to the kingside instead. In the extremely tense and complicated struggle which ensued, watching grandmasters had the greatest difficulty in assessing the position and explaining the myserious and provocative rook moves. First impressions suggested that Black had gained an advantageous position with two bishops and a potentially dangerous passed pawn, and it took long nights of hard analysis to discover Karpov's decisive error. As grandmasters dissected the tactics, Mikhail Botvinnik's comment from his Moscow apartment was that "Kasparov played perfectly".

**Kasparov-Karpov**
*Ruy Lopez*

| | | | | |
|---|---|---|---|---|
| 1 | e4 | *00* | e5 | *00* |
| 2 | ♘f3 | *00* | ♘c6 | *00* |
| 3 | ♗b5 | *01* | a6 | *00* |
| 4 | ♗a4 | *01* | ♘f6 | *01* |
| 5 | 0-0 | *01* | ♗e7 | *01* |
| 6 | ♖e1 | *01* | b5 | *01* |
| 7 | ♗b3 | *01* | d6 | *01* |
| 8 | c3 | *01* | 0-0 | *01* |
| 9 | h3 | *01* | ♗b7 | *04* |
| 10 | d4 | *01* | ♖e8 | *04* |
| 11 | ♘bd2 | *01* | ♗f8 | *05* |
| 12 | a4 | *07* | h6 | *08* |

Game 5 of the 1985 match had continued 12 ... ♕d7 13 ab ab 14 ♖xa8 ♗xa8 15 d5 ♘a5 16 ♗a2 c6 17 b4 ♘b7 18 c4 ♖c8 19 dc ♕xc6 and now White went wrong with

88

20 c5?!, going on to lose in 41 moves.

**13 ♗c2    09    ed    10**

In the 9th game of the same match Karpov preferred 13 ... ♘b8 14 ♗d3 c6 15 ♘f1 ♘bd7 16 ♘g3, when Black had a solid position. With the text Black takes up the challenge of a theoretical battle.

**14 cd    09    ♘b4    10**
**15 ♗b1    09    c5    13**
**16 d5    12    ♘d7    15**
**17 ♖a3    19**

This is superior to 17 ♘f1 f5 18 ef ♘f6, De Firmian-Belyavsky, Tunis IZ 1985.

**17 ...    c4    21**

**18 ab    35**

A novelty. The game Sokolov-Psakhis, Volgograd 1985, had continued 18 ♘d4 ♘e5 19 ab ♕b6! 20 ♘2f3 ♘ed3 21 ♗e3 (if 21 ♖e2 then 21 ... ab is fine for Black) 21 ... ♘xe1 22 ♘xe1 ♕c7 and Psakhis stood better.

**18 ...    ab    21**
**19 ♘d4    36    ♖xa3    23**

19 ... ♕b6 is answered by 20 ♘2f3.

**20 ba    37    ♘d3    23**
**21 ♗xd3    39    cd    26**
**22 ♗b2    59**

The speed with which Karpov was playing suggested that Kasparov's TN was nothing new to him. But after the text the Challenger sank into thought for 41 minutes.

Kasparov probably rejected 22 ♘xb5 on the grounds that after 22 ... ♗a6 23 a4 Black gets dangerous play with 23 ... ♗xb5! 24 ab ♕a5 25 ♘c4 ♕b4.

**22 ...    ♕a5    67**

Making it difficult to attack the d-pawn, as 23 ♘db3 ♕a4 24 ♕xd3 allows 24 ... ♗xd5.

**23 ♘f5    88**

With the powerful threat of 24 ♗xg7 and 25 ♕g4. 23 ...g6 fails to 24 ♘b3 ♕a4 25 ♕xd3! gf 26 ♕g3+ ♔h7 27 ♕f3 ♘e5 28 ♕xf5+ ♔g8 29 ♖e3 with an enormous attack, e.g. 29 ... ♗g7 30 ♖g3 ♘g6 31 ♗xg7 ♔xg7 32 ♕d7 winning.

**23 ...    ♘e5    84**
**24 ♗xe5!    94**

Original and brilliant. Kasparov cedes the bishop pair and allows Black to achieve a dangerous outside passed pawn on the queenside. In exchange White's d-pawn also becomes passed and he has latent threats on the kingside with his queen and knights.

24 f4 gets nowhere, except after

24 ... ♘c4? 25 ♘xc4 bc 26 ♗xg7! ♗xg7 27 ♕g4 ♕e1+ 28 ♔h2 ♕c3 29 e5. Instead Black has the solid 24 ... ♘g6, when 25 ♖f1 allows 25 ... ♖c8 26 ♘b3 ♕a4 27 ♕xd3 b4 28 ♖a1 (not 28 ♕g3 ba 29 ♗xg7 ♗xg7 30 ♘xg7 ♔xg7 31 f5 ♕xe4 32 fg ♕xg6) 28 ... ♘xf4 29 ♕f3 ♖c2, according to the Soviet master K.Asayev in the special match bulletin of the Tchigorin club.

**24 ...        de        96**

24 ... ♖xe5 25 ♘f3 ♖xf5 26 ef ♗xd5 also comes into consideration but White has very good winning chances after 27 ♖e3 ♗c4 28 f6, driving a wedge into the kingside.

**25 ♘b3    98    ♕b6!    121**

After 25 ... ♕xa3 26 ♕xd3 ♕b4 27 ♖b1 Black's queen is misplaced. With the text Karpov waits to capture the a-pawn with a rook or bishop.

**26 ♕xd3    101    ♖a8    122**

At first glance Black seems to be better. He will capture on a3 and push the b-pawn. In particular, White's knight on b3 appears to have nowhere to go. But Kasparov's next move lures the Challenger into capturing with the wrong piece.

**27 ♖c1!    129**

The start of a brilliant plan designed to break the co-ordination of Black's forces.

**27 ...        g6        125**

Karpov decides to dislodge the knight from its outpost where it is eyeing the d6 square. If 27 ... ♗xa3 28 ♕g3 wins. But 27 ... ♖xa3 is possible, e.g. 28 ♕c2 b4 29 ♘e3 ♗a6. Writing in the Leningrad bulletin, K.Asayev suggests the dangerous alternative 28 d6. 28 ... ♗xe4 now fails to 29 ♕xe4 ♖xb3 30 ♘e7+ ♔h8 31 ♖c8. Against 28 ... ♖a2 he gives 29 ♘c5 (one of the points of any d6 advance is that White gains control of c5) 29 ... g6 30 ♘e7+ ♔g7 (30 ... ♔h7 31 ♕b3) 31 ♕g3. Finally, if 28 ... ♖a8 29 ♘c5 ♖c8 30 ♘e7+ ♗xe7 31 de.

**28 ♘e3    132    ♗xa3?    128**

Karpov mistakenly allows his bishop to be lured to a3. The best defence is 28 ... ♖xa3 29 ♘g4 f6 30 ♕f3 ♖a6!, and now 31 d6 ♕xd6 32 ♘c5 ♖c6 33 ♕b3+ fails to 33 ... ♔g7 34 ♕xb5 ♗c8. Here White can only gain a minimal endgame edge with 32 ♕xb5 ♗xe4 33 ♕c4+ ♗d5 34 ♘xf6+ ♕xf6 35 ♕xd5+ ♕f7.

Asayev had a lot of fun with lines after 28 ... ♖xa3 29 ♘g4 ♗g7, investigating some intricate "knightmare" variations in which White's cavalry gallop around the board with impunity, e.g. 30 d6 h5 31 d7 ♖a8 32 ♘c5 ♗c6 33 ♘e3 ♗f8 34 ♘d5 ♕d5 35 ♘e6! fe 36 ♖xc6 ed 37 ♕xd5+ ♔g7 38 ♕e5+ ♔h7 39 ♕e6 ♔g5 40 ♖c8 and wins. An entertaining fantasy variation, but of course Black should play

30 ... ♖a6, with no serious problems.

**29 ♖a1** *134* **♖a4** *138*

If 29 ... h5 Suetin gives 30 ♕c3 ♕d6 31 ♘a5!. Perhaps Black must play 29 ... ♗f8, but 30 ♖xa8 ♗xa8 31 ♕c3 is unappetising.

**30 ♘g4** *136* **♗f8** *138*
**31 ♖c1** *138*

Of course not 31 ♘xe5 ♖xa1+ 32 ♘xa1 ♕f6 33 ♕g3 ♗g7 34 f4 g5. At this point Kasparov took off his watch for the ensuing time scramble.

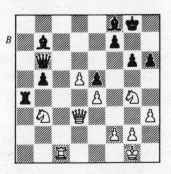

**31 ...** **♕d6?** *146*

Voluntarily relinquishing c5. After the game the authors received a telex from the London match centre at the Great Eastern Hotel suggesting 31 ... f6 32 ♕f3 ♖a6, transposing into the analysis after 28 ... ♖xa3. But this time White has an elegant forcing varition with 32 d6! ♕xd6 33 ♕xb5 ♖b4 34 ♕e8! and now:

a) 34 ... ♕e7 35 ♕xg6+ ♕g7 36 ♕e8 ♖xb3 37 ♕e6+ ♕f7 38 ♘xf6+ ♔g7 39 ♖c7 ♕xc7 40 ♘e8+.

b) 34 ... ♖xb3 35 ♕g6+ ♗g7 (35 ... ♔h8 36 ♘xf6) 36 ♘xh6+.

c) 34 ... ♗xe4 35 ♘c5 ♖b1 (35 ... ♗f5 36 ♘xh6+) 36 ♘e6.

d) 34 ... f5 35 ♘xe5 intending ♕f7+ and ♘xg6+.

White only has time for these variations because of the tempo gained against the rook on a4.

**32 ♘c5** *147*

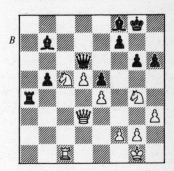

Now Karpov is forced into a lost ending.

**32 ...** **♖c4** *147*

If 32 ... ♖a7 33 ♕xb5.

**33 ♖xc4** *147* **bc** *147*
**34 ♘xb7** *147*

For a moment the crowd's attention was distracted as the losing 34 ♕xc4?? was played by one of the demonstrators, who quickly realised his mistake.

**34 ...** **cd** *147*
**35 ♘xd6** *147* **♗xd6** *147*
**36 ♔f1** *148* **♔g7** *147*
**37 f3** *148* **f5** *148*
**38 ♘f2** *148*

Forcing the pawn on to the

hopelessly exposed d2 square.

| 38 | ... | | d2 | 148 |
|----|-----|-----|-----|-----|
| 39 | ♔e2 | 148 | ♗b4 | 148 |
| 40 | ♘d3 | 149 | ♗c3 | 148 |
| 41 | ♘c5 | 153 | (sealed) | |

The next day Karpov **resigned** without resuming. One winning line goes 41 ... ♔f6 42 ♘b3 ♔g5 43 ♘xd2 ♔f4 44 ♔d3 ♗b4 45 ♘c4. If Black plays passively then White's knight will go to e6, eventually picking off another pawn.

Black lost both his d-pawns in this game, and White played ♘c5 twice – the first time it destroyed the Black position, the second it forced resignation!

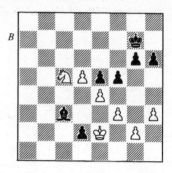

| Kasparov | ½ ½ ½ 1 0 ½ ½ 1 ½ ½ ½ ½ ½ 1 | 8 |
|----------|------------------------------|---|
| Karpov | ½ ½ ½ 0 1 ½ ½ 0 ½ ½ ½ ½ ½ 0 | 6 |

92

# GAME FIFTEEN, 12 September

After the efforts of the 14th game Kasparov took his second time-out, a clever decision as he went on in game 15 to draw easily with the black pieces.

After playing his 29th move in an equal ending with bishops of opposite colour Kasparov strode up and down on the stage seemingly without a care in the world. As he came back to the board Karpov looked up and offered a draw, which was accepted immediately.

In the opening Karpov used a line against the Grünfeld which had not been seen at world championship level since the Botvinnik-Petrosian match of 1963. After Karpov's aggressive central thrust it was Kasparov who produced a novelty, retreating his knight to an unlikely square. FIDE President Campomanes, dressed in a black tracksuit, made a visit to the telex area in the hotel and stayed for more than half an hour as journalists discussed the innovation. In fact Karpov took only four minutes over his reply to the opening surprise, temporarily winning a pawn. But Black was able to safeguard the rest of his queenside and eventually won White's vulnerable e-pawn in return.

At the time grandmasters were full of praise for Kasparov's "masterly" handling of the opening and not for one minute did anyone suggest that there might be a hole in his preparation.

**Karpov-Kasparov**
*Grünfeld Defence*

| | | | | |
|---|---|---|---|---|
| 1 | d4 | 00 | ♘f6 | 01 |
| 2 | c4 | 00 | g6 | 01 |
| 3 | ♘c3 | 00 | d5 | 01 |
| 4 | ♘f3 | 00 | ♗g7 | 01 |
| 5 | ♕b3 | 00 | | |

One of the most remarkable things about a world title contest is the way the participants keep finding new ways to test their opponent in the openings. Here Karpov rehabilitates the old "Russian System", last seen in the world championship match between Botvinnik and Petrosian, and after playing his "novelty" he began to stride confidently about the stage.

| | | | | |
|---|---|---|---|---|
| 5 | ... | | dc | 05 |
| 6 | ♕xc4 | 01 | 0-0 | 06 |
| 7 | e4 | 02 | ♗g4 | 07 |
| 8 | ♗e3 | 02 | | |

93

There was some annoyance in the audience with one of the demonstrators who left 8 ♗d3 on his board for half a minute.

| 8 | ... | | ♘fd7 | 07 |
| 9 | ♖d1 | 04 | ♘c6 | 08 |
| 10 | ♗e2 | 04 | ♘b6 | 09 |
| 11 | ♕c5 | 04 | | |

Karpov feels that 11 ♕b3 gets White nowhere.

| 11 | ... | | ♕d6 | 10 |
| 12 | e5 | 04 | | |

Flicked out so fast that some commentators were sure it must be new. Botvinnik-Fischer, Varna Olympiad 1962, had continued 12 h3 ♗xf3 13 gf ♖fd8 (13 ... e6!?) 14 d5 ♘e5 15 ♘b5 ♕f6 16 f4 ♘ed7 and Black stood well. 12 ♘b5 is also neutralised by 12 ... ♕xc5 13 dc ♘a4 14 b3 ♘c3 15 ♘xc3 ♗xc3+ – Alvarez-Uhlmann, Capablanca Memorial 1964.

| 12 | ... | | ♕xc5 | 29 |
| 13 | dc | 04 | ♘c8? | 30 |

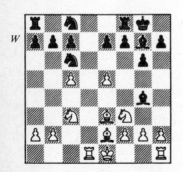

But this is the true innovation – in fact a very bad one, as we were

to find out in game 17. 13 ... ♘d7 is the usual continuation, but 14 h3! ♗xf3 15 gf is good for White since 15 ... ♘xe5 16 f4! wins. Karpov thought for only four minutes before playing

| 14 | ♘b5? | 08 | ♖b8 | 44 |

A clever reply, waiting for White to commit himself before deciding which way to capture on e5. 14 ... ♗xf3 15 ♗xf3 ♗xe5 allows White to penetrate with 16 ♖d7.

| 15 | ♘xc7 | 27 | e6 | 52 |

Another waiting move which simultaneously keeps the knight out of d5 and allows for a later ... ♘8e7-f5/d5. Kochiev gives 15 ... ♗xf3 16 ♗xf3 ♗xe5 17 ♖d7 ♗xb2 18 ♘a6 ba 19 ♗xc6, when c5 is defended and the knight on c8 has nowhere to go.

| 16 | ♘b5 | 67 | ♘8e7 | 55 |
| 17 | ♖d2 | 97 | | |

A typical Karpov rook move, defending b2 and giving possibilities of recapturing on e2 with the rook.

| 17 | ... | | b6 | 89 |

Fearing later attacks on his queenside pawns, Kasparov finds an original way of removing his weaknesses and undermining his opponent's control of d6. After 17 ... ♘d5 18 h3 ♗xf3 19 ♗xf3 ♘xe3 20 fe ♘xe5 21 ♘d6 White has the advantage.

| 18 | cb | 98 | ab | 90 |
| 19 | ♗g5 | 104 | ♘f5 | 103 |
| 20 | b3 | 110 | h6 | 111 |

| 21 | ♗f6 | 121 | ♗xf3 | 112 |
|----|------|-----|------|-----|
| 22 | ♗xf3 | 121 | ♘xe5 | 112 |
| 23 | ♗xe5 | 121 | ♗xe5 | 112 |

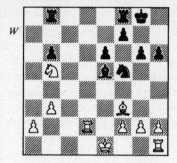

Black has completely equalised and White's queenside majority presents no danger.

| 24 | 0-0 | 124 | ♖fd8 | 131 |
|----|-----|-----|------|-----|

Kasparov decides there is little to be gained from pressing for anything more.

| 25 | ♖fd1 | 124 | ♖xd2 | 131 |
|----|------|-----|------|-----|
| 26 | ♖xd2 | 124 | ♖c8 | 131 |
| 27 | g3 | 124 | ♖c1+ | 132 |
| 28 | ♔g2 | 124 | ♔f8 | 132 |
| 29 | ♗e4 | 125 | ♔e7 | 134 |

**Draw Agreed**

| Kasparov | ½ ½ ½ 1 0 ½ ½ 1 ½ ½ ½ ½ ½ 1 ½ | 8½ |
|----------|---------------------------------|-----|
| Karpov | ½ ½ ½ 0 1 ½ ½ 0 ½ ½ ½ ½ ½ 0 ½ | 6½ |

# GAME SIXTEEN, 15 September

There were amazing scenes at the Hotel Leningrad as Kasparov took a three point lead, demolishing the former champion in a brilliant and hair-raising time scramble.

After a wildly complicated Ruy Lopez, some onlookers pronounced Kasparov's position dead as Karpov's rook penetrated on the queenside to win the trapped white knight. After playing his 32nd move Kasparov shifted nervously in his seat, alternately looking out into the audience and up at the lights above him. When he thought, he hunched his body down over the board with both legs shaking.

Finally Karpov realised the dangerous potential of White's forces gathered on the kingside, spending 29 minutes over his reply. As the players flashed out their moves Karpov's defences appeared to be holding. But then Kasparov unleashed a terrible pawn thrust, winning the black queen. As Kasparov's body visibly relaxed observers were stunned by what they saw as a total turnaround in the game's fortunes. As Karpov left himself with only one minute, the spectators became noisy, and after Kasparov snapped off the queen Karpov's tall blond girlfriend Natasha hurried out of the hall. Kasparov played his 41st move and began to make his way off stage. The audience stood and applauded as the Chief Arbiter Lothar Schmid stepped forward to demand silence by waving his hands in the air. After Kasparov had left the stage, Karpov signed his scoresheet, signalling resignation, and left the hotel. There was no handshake. Some of the audience began to move to the front of the stage, and when Kasparov returned to sign his own scoresheet there was another burst of applause. As he exited stage left for the second time Kasparov nodded triumphantly to a group of friends in the audience.

For the second time in a row Kasparov had hoodwinked the experts and had scored a remarkable victory with the white side of the Ruy Lopez. As the audience went for their coats and the journalists ran to the telexes, Soviet grandmasters began to talk openly of Karpov's chances as dead and of Kasparov as the new Fischer. With Karpov facing the monumental task of scoring four wins from the remaining eight games the match indeed seemed over and nobody could have predicted the dramatic twist of fortunes that was to take place over the next few games.

**Kasparov-Karpov**
*Ruy Lopez*

| | | | |
|---|---|---|---|
| 1 | e4 | 01 | e5 | 00 |
| 2 | ♘f3 | 01 | ♘c6 | 00 |
| 3 | ♗b5 | 01 | a6 | 00 |
| 4 | ♗a4 | 01 | ♘f6 | 00 |
| 5 | 0-0 | 01 | ♗e7 | 01 |
| 6 | ♖e1 | 01 | b5 | 01 |
| 7 | ♗b3 | 01 | d6 | 01 |
| 8 | c3 | 02 | 0-0 | 01 |
| 9 | h3 | 03 | ♗b7 | 02 |
| 10 | d4 | 03 | ♖e8 | 02 |
| 11 | ♘bd2 | 03 | ♗f8 | 03 |
| 12 | a4 | 05 | h6 | 03 |
| 13 | ♗c2 | 05 | ed | 04 |
| 14 | cd | 05 | ♘b4 | 04 |
| 15 | ♗b1 | 05 | c5 | 04 |
| 16 | d5 | 06 | ♘d7 | 05 |
| 17 | ♖a3 | 06 | c4 | 05 |
| 18 | ♘d4 | 09 | | |

So Kasparov is the first to diverge
from the 14th game. But Karpov's
camp have done their homework
and he comes up with an important
novelty.

| 18 | ... | ♕f6 | n.a. |
|---|---|---|---|

**19 ♘2f3 40**

To keep up the pressure against
b5. 19 ♘f5 g6 20 ♘g3 ♔h7 leaves
the knight misplaced.

| 19 | ... | ♘c5 | 12 |
|---|---|---|---|
| 20 | ab | 42 | ab | 13 |
| 21 | ♘xb5 | 58 | | |

This time Kasparov decides to
swipe off the b-pawn – a very confident decision given that Karpov
still seems to be in a prepared
line.

| 21 | ... | ♖xa3 | 14 |
|---|---|---|---|
| 22 | ♘xa3 | 60 | ♗a6 | 14 |
| 23 | ♖e3 | 64 | ♖b8 | 24 |
| 24 | e5 | 83 | | |

Also strong is the solid 24 ♘e1,
answering 24 ... g6 with 25 ♗d2
♕xb2? 26 ♗c3 ♕xa3 27 ♕d4. In
the press room, however, grandmasters had already suggested the
thrusting 24 e5 as far more in
keeping with Kasparov's style.

| 24 | ... | de | 26 |
|---|---|---|---|
| 25 | ♘xe5 | 85 | ♘bd3 | 88 |

As Kasparov rested backstage
Karpov pondered for 62 minutes.
In spite of the dangerous-looking
knights and his control of d3,
Black doesn't seem to have enough
for the pawn. Karpov must have
spent a long time checking that the
ending after 26 ♗xd3 ♘xd3 27
♖xd3 cd 28 ♘d7 ♕d8 29 ♘xb8
♕xb8 30 ♕a4 was just about holding. Better is 26 ... cd, when 27 ♘c6
♖b3 28 ♘a5 is equal.

| 26 | ♘g4 | 101 |
|---|---|---|

Rejecting the easy draw, Kasparov once again pulls out all the stops on the kingside. But after the game Khalifman and members of Kasparov's camp were agreed that 26 ♕c2 here would be crushing. The idea is simple – to defend f2, attack c4 and pile up on the b1-h7 diagonal. 26 ... ♘b3 allows 27 ♘d7, while 26 ... g6 is answered by 27 ♘axc4 ♗xc4 28 ♘xc4. The most testing line is 26 ... ♖b4 27 ♘c6 ♖b7 but then 28 ♖e8 with the idea of ♗e3xc5 leaves Black in knots.

**26 ...**      **♕b6**    *89*

Eyeing b2 and f2. 26 ... ♕d6 allows 27 ♖g3 ♔h8 28 ♘xh6 gh 29 ♕g4 ♕g6 30 ♕f3!.

**27 ♖g3**    *116*    **g6**    *94*

Perhaps it was time for the wild complications following from 27 ... ♘e4!? 28 ♘xh6+ ♔h7. After Karpov's choice Black seems to be about to crash through on the queenside.

**28 ♗xh6**    *131*    **♕xb2**    *101*

28 ... ♘e4 fails to 29 ♘xc4.

Another try is 28 ... ♘xf2!? 29 ♕d4 ♘xg4 30 ♗xf8 ♘d7.

**29 ♕f3**    *132*    **♘d7**    *110*

Black must defend f6 and there is no time for 29 ... ♕xa3 30 ♗xd3 ♘xd3 31 ♘f6+ ♔h8 32 ♕h5! with a massive attack.

**30 ♗xf8**    *134*    **♔xf8**    *117*

30 ... ♖xf8 is also risky – 31 ♗xd3 cd 32 ♘h6+ and now:

a) **32 ...** ♔g7 33 ♘f5+ ♔h7 34 ♕f4 ♕a1+ 35 ♔h2 ♕e5 36 ♕h6+ ♔g8 37 ♘h4 is dangerous.

b) **32 ...** ♔h7 33 ♘xf7 d2 34 ♘g5+ or 33 ... ♕xa3 34 ♕f4 give White good attacking chances – London bulletin.

**31 ♔h2!**    *138*

Brilliantly hiding the king away in preparation for the final attack.

**31 ...**      **♖b3**    *118*

Given an exclamation mark by some Soviet commentators, but maybe 31 ... ♕d4 is the only try. 31 ... ♕xa3 again fails to 32 ♘h6 ♕e7 33 ♖xg6 ♔e8 34 d6.

**32 ♗xd3**    *141*

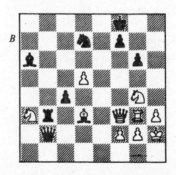

**32 ... cd?** *147*

By now Karpov's supporters had become nervous. Why had their man taken so long? Surely White's three-piece attack could be stopped.

In fact the text is a serious mistake. Confused by a plethora of captures Karpov misses 32 ... ♖xa3! 33 ♕f4 (33 ♕e2 ♕xe2 34 ♗xe2 ♖xg3 35 ♔xg3 c3! should hold for Black) 33 ... ♖xd3 34 ♕d6+ ♔g7 35 ♕xd7 ♖xg3 36 ♔xg3 c3 37 ♘e5 ♕b7 which holds the draw. But the ending after 32 ... ♖xd3 33 ♕f4 ♕xa3 34 ♘h6 ♕e7 35 ♖xg6 ♕e5 36 ♕xe5 ♘xe5 37 ♖xa6 ♖xd5 is probably winning for White.

**33 ♕f4** *142* **♕xa3** *149*

If 33 ... d2 IM Nikolai Popov gives 34 ♘h6 ♘f6 35 ♕d6+ ♔e8 36 ♕xa6 d1♕ 37 ♕c8+ ♔e7 38 ♕c5+ followed by ♘c4, claiming a White win.

**34 ♘h6** *143* **♕e7** *149*
**35 ♖xg6** *143* **♕e5** *149*
**36 ♖g8+** *143* **♔e7** *149*
**37 d6+!** *143*

Until this point the hall and the GM room had been waiting for a Karpov victory as the moves were flashed out in the time scramble. But this devastating shot blows the black defence away.

**37 ...** **♔e6** *149*

Playing on through inertia.

**38 ♖e8+** *143* **♔d5** *149*
**39 ♖xe5+** *143* **♘xe5** *149*
**40 d7** *144* **♖b8** *149*
**41 ♘xf7** *144* **Resigns**

As the crowd applauded the match seemed finished. Indeed many Soviet GMs began to talk of Kasparov wiping Karpov out and inching towards Fischer's magic 2780 rating.

| Kasparov | • | ½ | ½ | ½ | 1 | 0 | ½ | ½ | 1 | ½ | ½ | ½ | ½ | ½ | 1 | ½ | 1 | 9½ |
|----------|---|---|---|---|---|---|---|---|---|---|---|---|---|---|---|---|---|----|
| Karpov | | ½ | ½ | ½ | 0 | 1 | ½ | ½ | 0 | ½ | ½ | ½ | ½ | ½ | 0 | ½ | 0 | 6½ |

# GAME SEVENTEEN, 17 September

Just when everything seemed clear and commentators here are predicting a devastating Kasparov match victory, Karpov hits back with a crushing win to keep his chances alive. After his brilliant victory in the 16th game Kasparov seemed almost unrecognisable as he struggled in a hopeless ending.

Kasparov tempted fate by repeating the same opening idea as in game 15, but Karpov had used the five days wisely to come up with an elegant refutation. By move 17 Kasparov was close to lost, while Karpov had only used ten minutes of his time.

As journalists kept one eye on the video screens and Karpov rested backstage, Bob Walsh, the organiser of the 1990 Goodwill Games to be held in Seattle, announced at a press conference in the analysis room that chess would be included as a sport in the games.

Back at the board Karpov forced home his winning advantage with ruthless efficiency, and Kasparov had to resign shortly after move 30. As the audience applauded a middle-aged woman rushed forward with a bunch of carnations, presumably for the Challenger, but Karpov had left the stage by the time she had made her way to the front of the auditorium.

Many observers noted that Karpov had worn what appeared to be a new black suit for the game, a sign in earlier matches of his determination to go all out for a win.

A few days later the strangest incident occurred. A journalist was shown some of the goodwill telegrams arriving at the hotel for the two protagonists. One of the messages for Karpov came from a Soviet mystic. She had predicted that Karpov would win the 17th game and that this would prove to be a turning point in the match.

|   | **Karpov-Kasparov** | | | |
|---|---|---|---|---|
|   | *Grünfeld Defence* | | | |

| | | | | |
|---|---|---|---|---|
| 1 | d4 | 00 | ♘f6 | 00 |
| 2 | c4 | 00 | g6 | 00 |
| 3 | ♘c3 | 00 | d5 | 00 |

| | | | | |
|---|---|---|---|---|
| 4 | ♘f3 | 00 | ♗g7 | 01 |
| 5 | ♕b3 | 00 | dc | 09 |

For some minutes Kasparov hesitates before deciding to follow game 15.

| | | | | |
|---|---|---|---|---|
| 6 | ♕xc4 | 00 | 0-0 | 09 |

| 7 | e4 | 01 | ♗g4 | 09 |
|---|----|----|-----|----|
| 8 | ♗e3 | 02 | ♘fd7 | 09 |
| 9 | ♖d1 | 03 | ♘c6 | 09 |
| 10 | ♗e2 | 03 | ♘b6 | 09 |
| 11 | ♕c5 | 04 | ♕d6 | 09 |

In view of what happens perhaps Black should consider Pein's suggestion of 11 ... e6!?.

| 12 | e5 | 04 | ♕xc5 | 09 |
|----|----|----|------|----|
| 13 | dc | 04 | ♘c8 | 10 |

So far nothing new, but now Karpov produces a predictable but highly dangerous novelty.

| 14 | h3! | 05 |
|----|-----|----|

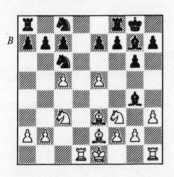

Sacrificing a pawn to force the knight on c8 into a straitjacket.

| 14 | ... | | ♗xf3 | 11 |
|----|-----|---|------|----|
| 15 | ♗xf3 | 05 | ♗xe5? | 20 |

Allowing White to realise his plan. It was rumoured that Kasparov's team had looked at this position on the morning of the game and concluded that 15 ... ♘xe5 was the only alternative here. A likely continuation is 16 ♗xb7 ♖b8 17 c6 (not 17 ♗xc8 ♖fxc8 to answer 18 ♘d5 with 18

... ♔f8) 17 ... ♘c4 18 ♖d7 ♘xb2 19 ♘b5 or 19 ♘d5 and White is better. Still, given what follows, it is very strange that Kasparov chose the bishop capture.

| 16 | ♗xc6 | 10 | bc | 20 |
|----|------|----|----|----|

16 ... ♗xc3+ 17 bc bc allows White the run of the black squares.

| 17 | ♗d4! | 10 |
|----|------|----|

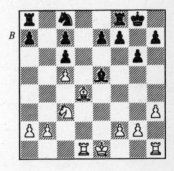

Taking Black's only active piece away from its best square.

| 17 | ... | | ♗f4 | 44 |
|----|-----|---|------|----|

Botvinnik suggested 17 ... ♗xd4 18 ♖xd4 ♖b8 19 b3 f5, but no one was able to find an answer to the simple 20 ♖d7 and 21 0-0.

The M.I.Chigorin Club bulletin gives the more sensible 17 ... ♗xd4 18 ♖xd4 a5 as a possibility, and White has to be careful here in order to keep his big advantage, for example 19 ♖d7 ♖b8 20 b3 ♘a7 21 ♖xc7 ♘b5 22 ♘xb5 ♖xb5 when 23 ♖xc6 allows the spoiling 23 ... a4.

| 18 | 0-0 | 15 | a5 | 71 |
|----|-----|----|----|----|

In the press room Khalifman

and Kochiev were suggesting 18 ... e5 as Black's only try. Things work out well after 19 ♗e3 ♗xe3 20 fe ♘e7 21 ♖d7 ♘f5 22 ♖xc7 ♖fc8, but Karpov has 22 ♔f2! ♖fd8 23 ♖fd1 ♖xd7 24 ♖xd7 winning. The solid 22 ♔f2 ♖ac8 also fails to 23 ♘e4! ♘g7 (playing for ... ♘e6 and ... ♖fd8) 24 ♘f6+ ♔h8 25 ♔e2 ♘e6 26 ♖e7 ♘xc5 27 b4 ♘e6 28 ♘d7 ♖fe8 29 ♖fxf7.

| 19 | ♖fe1 | 27 |
|----|------|----|

To discourage ... e5.

| 19 | ... | a4 | 79 |
|----|-----|----|----|
| 20 | ♖e4 | 41 | ♗h6 | 82 |
| 21 | ♗e5 | 42 | a3 | 82 |
| 22 | b3 | 42 | ♘a7 | 99 |
| 23 | ♖d7 | 48 | | |

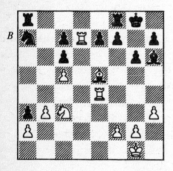

The culmination of Karpov's plan, whereby he will eventually pick up both of the c-pawns. His pieces are dominant, and the advance of the a-pawn mirrors the Champion's attempts to muddy the waters back in game 5. But by now even his own seconds were describing his position as hopeless.

| 23 | ... | ♗c1 | 114 |
|----|-----|-----|-----|
| 24 | ♖xc7 | 64 | | |

The most accurate. 24 ♖xe7 ♗b2 25 ♖xc7 fails to 25 ... ♗xc3 and 26 ... ♘b5.

| 24 | ... | ♗b2 | 118 |
|----|-----|-----|-----|
| 25 | ♘a4 | 75 | ♘b5 | 120 |
| 26 | ♖xc6 | 76 | ♖fd8 | 120 |
| 26 | ♖b6! | 88 | ♖d5 | 122 |
| 28 | ♗g3 | 93 | ♘c3 | 133 |
| 29 | ♘xc3 | 94 | ♗xc3 | 133 |
| 30 | c6 | 97 | ♗d4 | 133 |
| 31 | ♖b7 | 97 | | |

Having passed move 30, Kasparov decides to call it a day.

| 30 | ... | Black Resigns |
|----|-----|---------------|

The c-pawn is unstoppable.

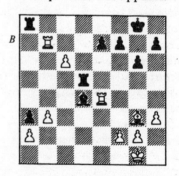

| Kasparov | ½ ½ ½ 1 0 ½ ½ 1 ½ ½ ½ ½ ½ ½ 1 ½ 1 0 | 9½ |
|----------|-------------------------------------|-----|
| Karpov | ½ ½ ½ 0 1 ½ ½ 0 ½ ½ ½ ½ ½ 0 ½ 0 1 | 7½ |

# GAME EIGHTEEN, 19 September

Karpov's dramatic fightback continues with a second consecutive victory after Kasparov self-destructs in time trouble in a clearly winning position.

Indeed Kasparov played the first part of the game brilliantly and gave every impression of having recovered from his debacle two days earlier. With a fine series of queen and rook manoeuvres he built up a tremendous kingside attack, but only at the cost of almost all his remaining time. As the complications increased there was a continuous whispering in the hall, while in the GM room an enormous crowd formed around Mark Taimanov and Alexei Suetin as they analysed.

Kasparov rejected a draw by repetition, but this show of bravado came horribly unstuck in the last few minutes of play. Kasparov missed two winning continuations and suddenly it was Karpov who had turned the tables and had a dangerous attack against the exposed white king.

As Kasparov sealed it was clear that all the chances were with Black, but when play resumed Karpov arrived nine minutes late, an almost sure sign his team were having trouble finding a rock hard win.

As Black's rooks and phalanx of pawns began to surround the white king Kasparov threw his queenside pawns up the board. But the black pawn mass continued on its deadly path and after his 57th move Karpov stood proudly behind his chair, his hands folded, rocking on his toes. Kasparov failed to find the one continuation that still tested Black, and was forced to resign when Karpov's 58th forced a beautiful picturebook mating finish. Karpov's delighted supporters in the hall rose to give the former Leningrad student a standing ovation, and he left the stage to wild and enthusiastic cheering.

**Kasparov-Karpov**
*Nimzo-Indian Deferred*

| | | | | |
|---|---|---|---|---|
| 1 | d4 | 00 | ♘f6 | 00 |
| 2 | c4 | 00 | e6 | 00 |
| 3 | ♘f3 | 00 | b6 | 02 |

Fresh from his victory Karpov avoids the stodgy Queen's Gambit.

| | | | | |
|---|---|---|---|---|
| 4 | ♘c3 | 01 | ♗b4 | 03 |
| 5 | ♗g5 | 01 | ♗b7 | 04 |
| 6 | e3 | 02 | h6 | 06 |
| 7 | ♗h4 | 02 | ♗xc3+ | 06 |

Karpov steers clear of 7 ... g5 8 ♗g3 ♘e4 9 ♕c2 ♗xc3+ 10 bc d6 11 ♗d3 f5 12 d5 and the Kasparov-Timman games from Hilversum

103

(see pages 21-23).

| 8 | bc | 02 | d6 | 06 |
|---|---|---|---|---|
| 9 | ♘d2 | 03 | g5 | 07 |
| 10 | ♗g3 | 03 | ♕e7 | 07 |
| 11 | a4 | 29 | | |

The start of an excellent plan to discourage long castling and undermine the queenside pawns.

| 11 | ... | | a5 | 11 |
|---|---|---|---|---|

Perhaps played a little hastily. 11 ... ♘c6 with the idea of 12 ... ♘a5 deserved serious consideration.

| 12 | h4 | 34 | ♖g8 | 11 |
|---|---|---|---|---|
| 13 | hg | 35 | hg | 11 |
| 14 | ♕b3! | 36 | | |

Messing up Black's development as 14 ... ♘bd7 blocking off the queen from c7 allows 15 c5.

| 14 | ... | | ♘a6 | 41 |
|---|---|---|---|---|

This leaves the knight dangerously out of play. 14 ... ♗c6, keeping open the option of 15 ... ♘bd7, might be stronger.

| 15 | ♖b1 | 59 | | |
|---|---|---|---|---|

Yet more prophylaxis against 15 ... 0-0-0. If Black castles White strikes out with 16 c5 dc 17 ♘c4 with the double threat of 18 ♘xb6 and 18 ♘xa5.

| 15 | ... | | ♔f8 | 61 |
|---|---|---|---|---|
| 16 | ♕d1! | 83 | | |

Combined with Kasparov's next move this sets in motion a very deep attacking idea. Having taken care of the queenside for the moment White regains control of the d1-h5 diagonal.

Yudasin mentions the possibility of 16 ♕c2 ♖e8 17 e4 e5 18 f3 ed

19 cd ♘b4.

| 16 | ... | | ♗c6 | 67 |
|---|---|---|---|---|
| 17 | ♖h2! | 94 | | |

Kasparov has placed Black in a kind of zugzwang, waiting for Karpov to commit his pieces before proceeding with the attack. The text also has the concrete intention of protecting g2 to free the light-squared bishop.

| 17 | ... | | ♔g7 | 97 |
|---|---|---|---|---|

In the special Leningrad bulletin the Soviet master K.Asayev analyses 17 ... ♕d7, which gangs up on the a-pawn and frees e7 as an alternative haven for the king: 17 ... ♕d7 18 ♗d3 ♔e7 (not 18 ... ♗xa4 19 ♕f3 ♔e7 20 ♖h6) 19 ♕e2 ♖h8 20 ♖xh8 ♖xh8 21 c5 ♖h1+ leaves Black with a lot of counterplay, but Asayev suggests 19 f3 ♗xa4 20 ♕e2 ♘b8 21 e4 as White's best continuation.

| 18 | c5! | 97 | | |
|---|---|---|---|---|

Sacrificing a pawn to open the diagonals for both white bishops.

| 18 | ... | | bc | 98 |
|---|---|---|---|---|

If 18 ... dc 19 ♗e5 ♔f8 20 ♗b5

♗b7 21 ♖h6 is most uncomfortable for Black.

| | | | | | |
|---|---|---|---|---|---|
| **19** | **♗b5** | *98* | **♘b8** | *108* | |

19 ... ♗xb5 is perilous on account of 20 ab ♘b8 21 dc.

| | | | | | |
|---|---|---|---|---|---|
| **20** | **dc** | *114* | **d5** | *1|2* | |
| **21** | **♗e5** | *121* | **♔f8** | *112* | |
| **22** | **♖h6** | *128* | **♘e8** | *114* | |

Black is forced to tie himself up in knots on the first and second ranks. 22 ... ♘fd7 loses to 23 ♗xc7 ♘xc5 24 ♗xb8, but despite the jumble of pieces Kasparov must play accurately to crack open the defensive wall.

| | | | | | |
|---|---|---|---|---|---|
| **23** | **♕h5** | *135* | **f6** | *115* | |

Essential. 23 ... ♗xb5 is busted by 24 ♖h7 ♗d3 25 ♕h6+ ♔g7 26 ♖xg7 ♖xg7 27 ♗xg7+ ♔e8 28 ♕h8+ ♔d7 29 ♕xb8.

| | | | | | |
|---|---|---|---|---|---|
| **24** | **♖h7** | *134* | **♘g7** | *122* | |
| **25** | **♕f3** | *134* | **♔f7** | *122* | |
| **26** | **♕h5+** | *142* | **♔f8** | *122* | |
| **27** | **♕f3** | *142* | **♔f7** | *122* | |

W

By now Kasparov had only eight minutes left on his clock. Given his two point lead the sensible course would surely have been to take the draw by repetition. Of course, if Kasparov had gone on to score a beautiful victory his bravado would have been universally applauded, but to continue in such a double-edged position and with so little time invites the Russian expression *nye nada* – "not necessary".

| | | | | | |
|---|---|---|---|---|---|
| **28** | **♖h6** | *142* | **♘e8** | *122* | |
| **29** | **e4** | *144* | | | |

In the analysis room GMs waited for 29 c4, which seems to be superior. For example, 29 ... ♗xb5 30 cd ♗d3 (not 30 ... ed 31 ♕xd5+ ♔g7 32 ♕xa8 ♔xh6 33 ♖xb5) 31 d6 cd 32 cd ♕d8 33 ♖b7+ ♘d7 34 ♕c6, or 29 ... ♘d7 30 ♗xc6 ♘xe5 31 ♕h5+. Black's best try is 29 ... g4, but after 30 ♖h7+ ♖g7 (30 ... ♘g7 loses to 31 ♕f4 ♗xb5 32 ♖xb5 ♘d7 33 ♗c3) 31 ♖xg7+ ♘xg7 32 ♕f4 ♗xb5 33 ♖xb5 ♘d7 34 ♗c3 White keeps the advantage.

| | | | | | |
|---|---|---|---|---|---|
| **29** | **...** | | **g4** | *127* | |
| **30** | **♕f4** | *144* | **♗xb5** | *127* | |
| **31** | **♖xb5** | *146* | **♘d7** | *132* | |
| **32** | **♗xc7** | *147* | | | |

B

32 ♗xf6 ♘exf6 33 e5 ♘xe5 34 ♕xe5 is also dangerous, but after the text Black can force a draw.

**32 ...        ♘xc5?   137**

Threatening the big fork on d3, but vastly inferior to 32 ... e5 33 ♕f5 ♘xc7, when White must take a draw with 34 ♕h5+ ♔f8 35 ♖h7 ♖g7 36 ♖h8+ as if instead 34 ♖b7 Black can wriggle out with 34 ... ♘xc5 35 ♖xf6+ ♔e8.

| | | | |
|---|---|---|---|
| **33** | **♕e3** | *147* | **♘xe4**   *140* |
| **34** | **♘xe4** | *147* | **de**     *140* |
| **35** | **♗xa5** | *147* | **f5**     *143* |
| **36** | **♗b4** | *147* | |

After a remarkable tour the bishop has emerged to dominate the dark squares, while the white rooks, like the claws of a crab, threaten a pincer movement to snap the Black defences.

**36 ...        ♕d7   145**
**37 ♕d4   147   ♖a7   146**

Forced. 37 ... ♕xd4 allows 38 ♖b7+.

**38 ♖h7+?   148**
With three minutes left Kasparov's nerves begin to crack.

Perhaps the loss of the 17th game had affected him more than he realised.

38 ♗c5 would have left Black helpless as the rook is needed to protect the 7th rank, leaving the a-pawn immune.

Dorfman also suggested 38 ♕e5 as another winning continuation, in which White avoids exchanges to keep the black king trapped in a net.

**38 ...        ♘g7   146**
**39 a5?   148**

For the second time Kasparov misses 39 ♗c5, which still wins. But now after . . .

**39 ...        ♔g6!   146**

. . . White has two rooks unprotected. In fact 39 ... ♕xb5! 40 ♕xa7+ ♔g6 would give Black an even stronger attack than in the game.

**40 ♕xd7   149   ♖xd7   146**

And Karpov confidently left the stage, knowing that the position had turned. White's once mighty rooks are suddenly badly discoordinated and his king exposed. Suddenly, too, Black's pawn phalanx threatens to descend on the white king. As Karpov supporters began to discuss the position with renewed optimism, Kasparov spent thirteen minutes over sealing. Overnight analysis suggested that Black had good winning chances, but when Karpov came into the hall nine minutes late it suggested that his team had been analysing to the very last minute and perhaps they hadn't found a watertight winning plan.

Kasparov sealed

**41 ♖h4** *162*

– by far the best, aiming to slow down ... f4. The photocopied game scores revealed that Kasparov had in fact crossed out his original sealed move, which looked to be 41 ♖xg7+. This move, also suggested by GMs at the time of sealing, loses to 41 ... ♖gxg7 followed by 42 ... ♖h7 and pushing the kingside pawns.

| 41 | ... | | ♖gd8 | *154* |
|----|-----|------|------|-------|
| 42 | c4 | *162* | ♖d1+ | *154* |
| 43 | ♔e2 | *162* | ♖c1 | *154* |
| 44 | a6 | *174* | | |

Another plausible attempt is 44 ♗c5 ♖xc4 45 ♗e3 with the bishop resurfacing on the c1-h6 diagonal, where it supports the threat of ♖h6+ and guards the pawn when it reaches a7. After 45 ... ♖c2+ 46 ♔e1 ♘h5 doesn't work because of 47 ♖b6, and meanwhile Kasparov threatens to push the a-pawn.

| 44 | ... | | ♖c2+ | *155* |
|----|-----|------|------|-------|
| 45 | ♔e1 | *175* | ♖a2 | *156* |
| 46 | ♖b6 | *180* | ♖d3 | *175* |
| 47 | c5 | *201* | ♖a1+ | *190* |
| 48 | ♔e2 | *202* | ♖a2+ | *191* |

Despite having more time Karpov repeats the position, sensibly realising that the complications to come may require all his available seconds.

| 49 | ♔e1 | *203* | g3 | *192* |
|----|-----|------|------|-------|

This move is the lynchpin of Black's winning strategy, removing the obstacle to the advance of the black pawn army.

| 50 | fg | *203* | ♖xg3 | *193* |
|----|-----|------|------|-------|
| 51 | ♔f1 | *206* | | |

51 ♖h2 only temporarily defends the pawn, as ... f4-f3 is coming.

| 51 | ... | | ♖gxg2 | *193* |
|----|-----|------|-------|-------|
| 52 | ♗e1 | *206* | ♖gc2 | *194* |
| 53 | c6 | *207* | ♖a1 | *194* |
| 54 | ♖h3 | *208* | f4 | *200* |

54 ... ♘h5 and only then 55 ... f4 may be more accurate, removing all White's counterplay.

| 55 | ♖b4 | *208* | ♔f5 | *201* |
|----|-----|------|------|-------|

This allows White to gain a tempo against the black king, complicating Black's winning task. After 55 ... ♘f5 56 ♖xe4 ♘g3+ 57 ♖xg3 fg 58 ♖g4+ (or 58 ♖xe6+ ♔f5 59 ♖e8 g2) 58 ... ♔f5 59 ♖xg3 ♖xc6 White can resign.

| 56 | ♖b5+ | *209* | e5 | *202* |
|----|------|------|----|-------|

The king gets boxed in after 56 ... ♔g4 57 ♖h4+ ♔f3 58 ♖h3+.

| 57 | ♖a5 | *212* | | |

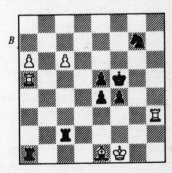

White is still fighting. He has been able to regroup his rook behind the a-pawn and threatens to marshall it home to a queen.

**57 ...                    ♖d1**    *222*

Karpov chooses what may be the more complicated way to win!

57 ... ♖xa5 58 ♗xa5 ♖xc6 59 a7 ♖a6 60 ♗b6 and 61 ♖h8 is no good for Black, and 57 ... ♖b1 allows 58 ♖b3, deflecting the black rook away from the 8th and the mates with ... e3 and ... ♖f2+.

But 57 ... ♖ac1 (paradoxical looking but winning a vital tempo) may be a more straightforward win than the text. In order to fend off mate White must deflect the rook with 58 c7 e3 59 ♖h2 ♖xc7 60 a7, but Black has 60 ... f3! threatening mate with 61 ... ♖xe1+ and ... ♖c1, and the attempted defence with 61 ♖e2 fails by one tempo after 61 ... fe+ 62 ♔xe2 ♖xa7 63 ♖xa7, and now Black succeeds in holding both e-pawns with 63 ... ♘e6.

**58   a7?**    *216*

Truly feeble. White can force his opponent to play accurately with 58 c7, when 58 ... e3 is not sufficient to win: 58 ♖a2! (but not 58 ♖h2? ♖xc7 60 a7 f3 61 ♖e2 when Black can win with 61 ... fe+ 62 ♔xe2 ♖d8 63 a8♕ ♖xa8 64 ♖xa8 ♔f4 keeping both pawns) 59 ... ♖xc7 60 a7 and Black does not have the try 60 ... f3, while if 59 ... ♖cc1 60 ♖xe3! fe 61 a7 ♖xe1+ 62 ♔g2 ♘e6 63 a8♕ e2!? 64 ♔f2! and Black cannot win.

Correct is 58 c7 ♖cc1! 59 a7 (59 c8♕ ♖xc8 60 a7 ♖a8 61 ♖b3 ♖d7 62 ♖bb5 ♔g4! 63 ♖xe5 ♔f3 64 ♖a4 e3 65 ♖ee4 ♘h5 wins) 59 ... ♖xe1+ 60 ♔f2 e3+ 61 ♖xe3 (forced) 61 ... fe+ 62 ♔f3 ♘e6! 63 a8♕ ♘g5+ 64 ♔g3 ♘e4+ winning the queen or mating.

**58   ...                    e3**    *224*
**White Resigns**

59 ♖f3 ♘h5 mates after 60 a8♕ ♘g3+ 61 ♖xg3 ♖f2+ and 62 ... ♖xe1. Another beautiful line goes 59 ♖f3 ♔e4 60 a8♕ ♔xf3 61 c7+ e4 and the king is protected by the black phalanx.

After Kasparov resigned Karpov received a standing ovation, and the former champion lingered on the stage, soaking up the applause to strengthen his confidence before the next game.

| | | | | | | | | | | | | | | | | | | | | |
|---|---|---|---|---|---|---|---|---|---|---|---|---|---|---|---|---|---|---|---|---|
| **Kasparov** | ½ | ½ | ½ | 1 | 0 | ½ | ½ | 1 | ½ | ½ | ½ | ½ | ½ | 1 | ½ | 1 | 0 | 0 | | 9½ |
| **Karpov** | ½ | ½ | ½ | 0 | 1 | ½ | ½ | 0 | ½ | ½ | ½ | ½ | ½ | 0 | ½ | 0 | 1 | 1 | | 8½ |

# GAME NINETEEN, 24 September

With a third successive victory Karpov completes a brilliant recovery to equal the match score. For the second time in a row he achieves a crushing position against the Grünfeld, producing an extremely dangerous new move against the double-edged Prins System.

Kasparov sacrificed the exchange for a pawn to activate his pieces, but the Black counterplay never got off the ground and Karpov was able to return the material to reach an easily winning ending. The next day Kasparov resigned without resuming.

**Karpov-Kasparov**
*Grünfeld Defence*

| | | | | | | | | |
|---|---|---|---|---|---|---|---|---|
| 1 | d4 | 00 | ♘f6 | 01 |
| 2 | c4 | 00 | g6 | 01 |
| 3 | ♘c3 | 00 | d5 | 01 |
| 4 | ♘f3 | 00 | ♗g7 | 01 |
| 5 | ♕b3 | 01 | dc | 02 |
| 6 | ♕xc4 | 01 | 0-0 | 02 |
| 7 | e4 | 01 | ♘a6 | 02 |

The Prins System has a rather risky reputation at GM level. Given the speed of Karpov's response, he must have been very well prepared for it. There were those who questioned the wisdom of Kasparov's choice since it is the obvious replacement if the Smyslov System is shot down.

**8  ♗e2  04**

The simplest and clearest line.

**8  ...  c5  02**

**9  d5  04**

Of course, 9 dc ♗e6 10 ♕b5 ♖c8 allows strong counterplay.

| | | | | | |
|---|---|---|---|---|---|
| 9 | ... | | e6 | 02 |
| 10 | 0-0 | 05 | ed | 02 |
| 11 | ed | 05 | ♗f5 | 03 |

After 11 ... ♘e8 12 ♗g5 f6 13 ♗f4 ♖f7 14 ♖ad1 was good for White in Szabo-Wade, Trencianske Teplice 1949.

**12  ♗f4!  08**

The new main line. The old move was 12 a3.

**12  ...  ♖e8  08**

12 ... ♕b6 is the main alternative and after this débâcle will probably become the main line:

a) **13 ♕b5 ♕xb5 14 ♗xb5 ♘b4 15 ♖ad1** a6 with good chances.

b) **13 ♖ad1 ♕xb2 14 ♘h4 ♘e4 15 ♘a4 ♕f6** = Chernin-Gavrikov, match (Soviet Championship play-off) 1985.

c) **13 ♗e5** is given '!' by Lebredo in *Informator* 41. Now 13 ... ♕xb2 14 ♘e4 ♕b6 15 ♗xf6! ♗xf6 16 ♖b1 is good for White, but Pein suggests 13 ... ♕b4 (13 ... ♖e8!?), intending

... ♛xc4 and ... ♞e8, as logical in view of White's omission of a3. This plan was used successfully in Hybl-Estrin, 6th World Correspondence Championship 1968-71. So what did Karpov intend?

**13 ♖ad1** *08* **♞e4** *09*

13 ... ♛b6 has a sounder theoretical reputation. After 14 ♛b5 Black's best is 14 ... ♝d7 15 ♛xb6 ab 16 ♞e5 ♞h5!, instead of 14 ... ♞b4 15 a3! ± Dlugy-Gavrikov, Tunis Interzonal 1985.

With the text Black appears to be forcing matters and gaining the upper hand in the centre, but now Karpov flashes out a startling reply which may refute the entire Black conception.

**14 ♞b5!!** *09*

Why has this not been played before? A natural reluctance to leave b2 hanging? But on closer inspection 14 ... ♝xb2 15 d6 looks devastating. Further virtues of Karpov's innovation are that it avoids exchanges and increases the power of White's passed pawn. In the press room Khalifman noted that

only 14 ♝e3 had been played in previous games, but then Black can entrench a knight on d6.

**14 ...** **♛f6** *30*

14 ... g5 15 ♝e3 ♝d7 16 d6 ♝xb5 17 ♛xb5 ♞xd6 18 ♛b3 g4 19 ♞g5 cedes White a huge number of threats according to Averbakh and Taimanov. Black's choice speculates on the unprotected state of White's bishop on f4.

**15 ♝d3** *15* **♞b4** *55*

This comes close to losing by force, but Black's two major alternatives both fail to the same reply:

a) **15 ... ♝g4** 16 ♝e5 ♖xe5 17 ♞xe5 ♝xd1 18 ♝xe4 ♛xe5 19 ♖xd1 and the a6 knight is misplaced for stopping the d-pawn.
b) **15 ... ♝d7** 16 ♝e5 ♖xe5 17 ♞xe5 ♛xe5 18 ♝xe4 ♝xb5 19 ♛xb5 ♛xe4 20 ♛xb7 wins.

Many players would be terrified by ... ♞b4 from Kasparov, but Karpov refuses to be bluffed.

**16 ♞c7** *37* **♞xd3** *82*
**17 ♞xe8** *40* **♖xe8** *82*
**18 ♛xd3** *41* **♛xb2** *83*

The best try. The tactical justification of Karpov's novelty lies in 18 ... ♞g3 19 ♛b5 winning. The respective clock times reveal that Kasparov was most dissatisfied with his position.

**19 ♖de1** *57*

Threatening 20 g4. The reckless 20 ♖fe1 fails to 20 ... ♛xf2+ 21 ♔h1 ♛xe1+ 22 ♖xe1 ♞f2+ 23

110

♔g1 ♖xe1+ 24 ♔xf2 ♗xd3. After White's choice the potential e-file pin will one day be decisive.

19 ... ♛b4 92

19 ... ♛xa2 allows 20 ♛b5!.

20 ♘d2! 82

Forcing a winning ending.

20 ... ♛a4 102

The only way to protect e8 and forestall 21 f3.

21 ♛c4 97 ♛xc4 105

22 ♘xc4 97 ♗c3 115

Taimanov suggests here 22 ... b5 23 ♘d2 ♘f6 24 ♖xe8+ ♘xe8 as Black's last chance.

23 ♘d2 107 ♗xd2 120

24 ♗xd2 107 ♗d7 121

Observers in the hall noted that Karpov seemed momentarily stunned by this resource. For over 30 seconds his hand hovered in the air, balancing his pen. But White's position is so good that after a further quarter of an hour Karpov found a crushing continuation.

24 ... ♖d8 would have failed to 25 ♗h6, shutting in the black king.

25 ♗f4! 123 ♗b5 123

26 f3 123

Returning the exchange to reach a victorious ending.

26 ... g5 126

26 ... ♗xf1 27 ♔xf1 ♘f6 28 ♖xe8+ ♘xe8 29 ♗e5! and Black loses his knight for the d-pawn.

27 ♗xg5 125 ♗xf1 128

28 ♔xf1 125 ♘d6 128

29 ♗e7 130

Once again Karpov displays lethal accuracy. Black would retain microscopic drawing chances after 29 ♖xe8+ ♘xe8 30 ♗e7 f5 31 ♗xc5 b6 32 ♗d4 ♔f7.

29 ... ♘c8 130

If 29 ... ♘c4 30 d6 ♘b6 31 ♖b1 and Black can resign.

30 ♗xc5 130 ♖d8 130

31 ♖e5 135 f6 130

32 ♖f5 135 b6 131

32 ... ♔f7 would have hung on a bit longer, though 33 g4 ♘e7 34 ♖h5 forces 34 ... ♖h8.

33 ♗d4 140 ♘e7 134

34 ♗xf6 141 ♖xd5 136

35 ♖g5+ 141 ♖xg5 137

36 ♗xg5 141 ♘c6 137

37 ♔e2 141 ♔f7 137

38 ♔d3 141 ♔e6 137

39 ♔c4 142 ♘e5+ ·137

40 ♔d4 143 ♘c6+ 138

41 ♔c4 150 (sealed)

It was no surprise the following day when Kasparov resigned without resuming. White's king can penetrate on either side and in such positions the bishop always outruns the knight. After seeming to have both feet in the grave Karpov had tied the match with the most remarkable string of victories in modern world championship play.

| | | | | | | | | | | | | | | | | | | | | |
|---|---|---|---|---|---|---|---|---|---|---|---|---|---|---|---|---|---|---|---|---|
| Kasparov | ½ | ½ | ½ | 1 | 0 | ½ | ½ | 1 | ½ | ½ | ½ | ½ | ½ | 1 | ½ | 1 | 0 | 0 | 0 | 9½ |
| Karpov | ½ | ½ | ½ | 0 | 1 | ½ | ½ | 0 | ½ | ½ | ½ | ½ | ½ | 0 | ½ | 0 | 1 | 1 | 1 | 9½ |

# GAME TWENTY, 29 September

After his elegant demolition of the Grünfeld in game 19 Karpov took a surprise time out, postponing the 20th until the following Monday. The decision mystified observers who had expected the former champion to keep pushing against a weakened Kasparov, but grandmasters suggested that Karpov wished to use the weekend to prepare himself psychologically for the final phase of the match now that he had gained real chance to win. Rumours that Karpov was ill were soon quashed that evening when Karpov was shown on Leningrad TV visiting an exhibition by the famous Soviet artist Ilya Glazunov with his girlfriend Natasha and close aide Vladimir Pischenko.

When he came to the board Kasparov employed a solid variation of the Catalan with the White pieces, and the game was drawn in only 21 moves.

Three correspondents from the *New York Times*, *Washington Post* and the *Financial Times* arrived from Moscow to write about the match, but in the middle of play came the news that *US News And World* reporter Nicholas Daniloff, accused of spying, had been allowed to leave the Soviet Union and was already on a plane to Germany. One journalist filed his Daniloff story from the match telex office but with so much news breaking the correspondents were obliged to return to Moscow the next evening, having witnessed only one short draw. A boring draw at that, but while some thought Kasparov had wasted one of his remaining whites, he had at least ended his disastrous run of losses.

### Kasparov-Karpov
*Catalan*

| | | | | |
|---|---|---|---|---|
| 1 | d4 | 00 | ♘f6 | 00 |
| 2 | c4 | 00 | e6 | 00 |
| 3 | g3 | 01 | | |

The Catalan is a common sanctuary when a draw with White is required against Karpov. Korchnoi switched to the Catalan in 1978 after his disaster in games 13 and 14, while Kasparov himself used the Catalan against Karpov for game 8 in 1984 after he had lost three of the first seven.

| | | | |
|---|---|---|---|
| 3 | ... | d5 | 00 |

112

| | | | |
|---|---|---|---|
| 4 | ♗g2 | 01 | ♗e7 | 01 |
| 5 | ♘f3 | 01 | 0-0 | 01 |
| 6 | 0-0 | 02 | dc | 3 |
| 7 | ♕c2 | 02 | a6 | 03 |
| 8 | ♕xc4 | 02 | b5 | 03 |
| 9 | ♕c2 | 02 | ♗b7 | 03 |
| 10 | ♗g5 | 02 | | |

10 ♗d2 ♘e4 11 ♕c1 ♗b7 was the above mentioned 8th game.

| | | | |
|---|---|---|---|
| 10 | ... | | ♘bd7 | 36 |
| 11 | ♗xf6 | 02 | ♘xf6 | 37 |
| 12 | ♘bd2 | 02 | ♖c8 | 44 |
| 13 | ♘b3 | 03 | c5 | 63 |
| 14 | dc | 05 | ♗d5 | 64 |
| 15 | ♖fd1 | 16 | ♗xb3 | 77 |

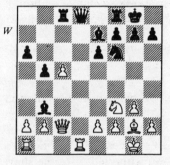

16 ♕xb3 24

If 16 ab ♖xc5 17 ♕xc5 ♗xc5! 18

♖xd8 ♖xd8 19 ♖xa6 ♖d1+ 20 ♗f1 g6 followed by ... ♘e4, Black generates sufficient counterplay. 17 ... ♕xd1+ 18 ♖xd1 ♗xc5 19 ♖c1! ♖c8 20 ♘d4 ♖c7 21 b4 ♗b6 22 ♖xc7 ♗xc7 23 ♗b7 is also probably a draw, but Black has more struggling to do.

| | | | |
|---|---|---|---|
| 16 | ... | | ♕c7 | 85 |
| 17 | a4 | 46 | ♕xc5 | 106 |
| 18 | ab | 49 | | |

If 18 ♘d4 ♖fd8 19 e3 e5 20 ♘f5 ♗f8 and White's knight is on the wrong track.

| | | | |
|---|---|---|---|
| 18 | ... | | ab | 107 |
| 19 | ♘d4 | 53 | | |

Or 19 ♖a5 ♘g4 20 ♘d4 ♗f6 21 ♖xb5 ♗xd4 22 ♖xc5 ♗xf2+ 23 ♔h1 ♗xc5 24 ♖f1 ♘f2+ draws.

| | | | |
|---|---|---|---|
| 19 | ... | | b4 | 108 |
| 20 | e3 | 67 | ♖fd8 | 109 |
| 21 | ♖d2 | 71 | ♕b6 | 113 |

**Drawn**

The final position looks completely level and there was no justification for Kasparov to speculate on Karpov's relative time shortage.

| Kasparov | ½ ½ ½ 1 0 ½ ½ 1 ½ ½ ½ ½ ½ 1 ½ 1 0 0 0 ½ | **10** |
|---|---|---|
| Karpov | ½ ½ ½ 0 1 ½ ½ 0 ½ ½ ½ ½ ½ 0 ½ 0 1 1 1 ½ | **10** |

# GAME TWENTY-ONE, 1 October

Kasparov again puts the brakes on Karpov with a professional defensive display which succeeds in splitting the point.

Kasparov wisely chose to play the super-solid Queen's Indian for the first time in the match. At first it seemed that Karpov had gained a significant edge, but by exchanging major pieces Kasparov reached a near equal ending.

With time running out in the match Karpov chose to soldier on, but in the second session a forcing line from Kasparov quickly led to a draw. For a few seconds, though, there was total confusion in the hall as Kasparov's final move appeared to have thrown away a piece. In reality the piece 'sac' was all home analysis leading to a dead draw.

So Kasparov had survived the big test with the black pieces. David Bronstein told Phil Walden of Reuters: "This result is very good for Kasparov, who should now go on to retain his title".

**Karpov-Kasparov**
*Queen's Indian Defence*

| 1 | d4 | 01 | ♘f6 | 00 |
| 2 | c4 | 01 | e6 | 00 |

The first time in the their 93 championship games that Kasparov has been willing to defend the black side of a Nimzo-Indian. Although he has defended with the Queen's Indian against Karpov before, it has never been via a move order which permits White to play 3 ♘c3 here.

| 3 | ♘f3 | 01 | b6 | 00 |
| 4 | g3 | 02 | ♗a6 | 01 |
| 5 | b3 | 04 | ♗b4+ | 04 |
| 6 | ♗d2 | 04 | ♗e7 | 04 |

| 7 | ♗g2 | 04 | 0-0 | 06 |
| 8 | 0-0 | 09 | d5 | 21 |
| 9 | ♘e5 | 24 | | |

Karpov follows Kasparov's own treatment when he had White in game 6 of their first match. In games 14 and 15 in 1984 White chose 9 cd ♘xd5 10 ♘c3 ♘d7 11 ♘xd5 ed 12 ♖c1.

| 9 | ... | | c6 | 27 |
| 10 | ♗c3 | 25 | ♘fd7 | 27 |
| 11 | ♘xd7 | 25 | ♘xd7 | 27 |
| 12 | ♘d2 | 25 | ♖c8 | 29 |

Yusupov has suggested here the prophylactic measure 12 ... f5.

| 13 | e4 | 30 | dc | 33 |
| 14 | bc | 35 | b5 | 34 |
| 15 | ♖e1 | 37 | | |

114

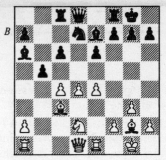

**15 ...        bc        37**

In game 6 from 1984 Karpov as Black tried 15 ... ♘b6, when 16 c5 would have given White the advantage, e.g. 16 ... ♘a4 17 ♕c2 e5 18 ♘f3 ♘xc3 19 ♕xc3 ed 20 ♘xd4 followed by 21 ♖ad1. Kasparov attempts to improve.

**16 ♕c2        42**

A more subtle idea is 16 ♕a4 ♗b5 17 ♕c2, which gives White the possibility of playing a4 with gain of tempo.

**16 ...        ♕c7        72**

Black's position looks passive and his extra pawn tends to block the action of his own pieces. At some point Black must try to liberate himself by means of either ... e5 or ... c5. The immediate 16 ... e5 looks dubious after 17 ♗h3 or 17 de ♘xe5 18 ♗f1 ♘d3 19 ♖ed1 threatening 20 ♘xc4. In the game Chernin-Hertneck, Lucerne (World Team Championship) 1985, Black's choice was 16 ... ♘b6, but after 17 ♘f1 c5 18 d5 White was still better. Kasparov did not look happy in this position but over the next few

moves he conceives an interesting plan to return his extra material and bring about simplification.

**17 ♘f1        62**

Karpov follows Chernin's example. Interesting alternatives are 17 ♗f1 and 17 ♖ad1.

| **17** | **...** | **e5** | **95** |
|---|---|---|---|
| **18** | **♘e3** | **63** | **ed** | **98** |
| **19** | **♗xd4** | **64** | **♗c5** | **98** |
| **20** | **♗xc5** | **70** | **♘xc5** | **99** |
| **21** | **♘xc4** | **70** | | |

White has regained his pawn and Black is saddled with an isolated pawn on the open c-file. If White were given time to consolidate, his advantage would become serious. However, regaining the pawn has cost White time and Black uses his slight lead in development to force a massive liquidation.

**21 ...        ♖fd8        104**

Black is now well coordinated and plans to invade with a knight on d3. This prompts Karpov to offer an exchange of rooks.

| **22** | **♖ad1** | **81** | **♖xd1** | **108** |
|---|---|---|---|---|
| **23** | **♖xd1** | **81** | **♖d8** | **108** |
| **24** | **♖xd8+** | **88** | **♕xd8** | **109** |
| **25** | **h4** | **89** | | |

To make *luft* for his king. Not 25 ♘e5? ♕d4 threatening ... ♕a1+.

**25 ...        ♕d4        111**

**26 ♕b2!        92**

White must exchange queens and does this by threatening ♕b8+.

| **26** | **...** | **♕xb2** | **114** |
|---|---|---|---|
| **27** | **♘xb2** | **94** | **f6** | **115** |
| **28** | **f3** | **110** | | |

If 28 f4 &f7 29 &f2 ♞d3+ with a draw. Karpov strengthens his pawn chain and tries to make use of the blockading square on c4. Nevertheless, with correct play the ending must be drawn.

| | | | |
|---|---|---|---|
| 28 | ... | &f7 | 117 |
| 29 | ♗f1 | 115 ♗b5 | 128 |
| 30 | &f2 | 117 &e6 | 132 |
| 31 | ♗c4 | 119 &d6 | 133 |
| 32 | &e3 | 122 ♞d7 | 137 |
| 33 | f4 | 123 ♞b6 | 139 |
| 34 | ♗g8 | 124 | |

Tempting a slight weakening of Black's pawns.

| | | | |
|---|---|---|---|
| 34 | ... | h6 | 140 |
| 35 | ♞d3 | 125 ♞d7 | 140 |
| 36 | &d4 | 136 c5+ | 142 |
| 37 | &c3 | 136 ♗c6 | 142 |

A main theme of Black's defence – counterplay against e4.

| | | | |
|---|---|---|---|
| 38 | ♞f2 | 137 ♞b6 | 145 |
| 39 | ♗b3 | 140 ♞a8 | 146 |
| 40 | &d3 | 141 ♞b6 | 146 |
| 41 | ♗c2 | 149 | |

B

| 41 | ... | ♗b5+ | 158 |
|---|---|---|---|

Kasparov sealed this active move. It may not appear that there are many dangers lurking in this simple position, but if Black is not careful White could still create an annoying offensive based on the transfer of his knight to f5. For example, if Black temporizes with 41 ... ♗d7 42 ♞d1 ♗c6 43 ♞e3 ♗d7 44 g4 ♗c8 45 ♗b3 ♗d7 46 ♞f5+ ♗xf5 47 gf. In this position White has excellent chances based on a combination of ♗e6, e5 and king penetration on the right flank. Black might still be able to draw by a timely advance of his passed pawn, but it would be an uphill struggle.

| 42 | &c3 | 150 ♞a4+ | 158 |
|---|---|---|---|
| 43 | &d2 | 151 | |

43 ♗xa4 ♗xa4 gets White nowhere. His e4 pawn will always be subject to attack by the bishop.

| 43 | ... | c4! | 158 |
|---|---|---|---|

As so often Kasparov refuses to defend passively. This aggressive thrust cuts right through the Gordian knot of White's advantage.

| 44 | e5+ | 158 fe | 159 |
|---|---|---|---|
| 45 | ♞e4+ | 158 &e6 | 159 |

**Drawn**

After 46 ♗xa4 ♗xa4 47 ♞c5+ &f5 48 ♞xa4 ef 49 gf &xf4 50 ♞c5 g5 White cannot win. A most unexpected conclusion for the onlookers but evidently the players trusted each other's analysis.

| Kasparov | ½ ½ ½ 1 0 ½ ½ 1 ½ ½ ½ ½ ½ 1 ½ 1 0 0 0 ½ ½ | 10½ |
|---|---|---|
| Karpov | ½ ½ ½ 0 1 ½ ½ 0 ½ ½ ½ ½ ½ 0 ½ 0 1 1 1 ½ ½ | 10½ |

# GAME TWENTY-TWO

After a virtuoso display of unrelenting positional pressure, Kasparov regains the lead with a dramatic and dazzling second session finale. As the audience rose for a standing ovation Kasparov and Karpov remained seated and exchanged some words. It was the first time the two protagonists had indulged in any kind of post mortem for 47 games.

**Kasparov-Karpov**
*Queen's Gambit Declined*

| 1 | d4 | 02 | ♞f6 | 00 |
|---|-----|-----|------|-----|
| 2 | c4 | 03 | e6 | 01 |
| 3 | ♞f3 | 03 | d5 | 02 |

We find this a strange decision at such a critical stage of the match. It is hard to play for a win on the Black side of a Queen's Gambit, while White can exert truly annoying long-term pressure. There is more fight in 3 ...b6 as he played in game 18 – the only Black win so far in this match.

| 4 | ♞c3 | 03 | ♝e7 | 02 |
|---|------|-----|------|-----|
| 5 | ♝g5 | 03 | h6 | 02 |
| 6 | ♝xf6 | 03 | ♝xf6 | 02 |
| 7 | e3 | 03 | 0-0 | 03 |
| 8 | ♖c1 | 04 | c6 | 03 |
| 9 | ♝d3 | 04 | ♞d7 | 04 |
| 10 | 0-0 | 04 | dc | 04 |
| 11 | ♝xc4 | 04 | e5 | 05 |

Game 12 saw 11 ... c5 from Karpov.

| 12 | h3 | 05 | ed | 05 |
|----|-----|-----|------|-----|
| 13 | ed | 06 | ♞b6 | 05 |

And here 13 ... c5 was played in game 10. Karpov was evidently dissatisfied with the course of both games and reverts to the method of defence he adopted in game 23 of their second match.

| 14 | ♝b3 | 06 | ♝f5 | 05 |
|----|------|-----|------|-----|

A nuance. 14 ... ♖e8 15 ♖e1 ♝f5 16 ♖xe8+ ♛xe8 17 ♛d2 was game 23 in 1985.

| 15 | ♖e1 | 06 | a5 | 06 |
|----|------|-----|------|-----|
| 16 | a3 | 13 | ♖e8 | 06 |
| 17 | ♖xe8+ | 15 | ♛xe8 | 06 |
| 18 | ♛d2 | 16 | ♞d7 | 06 |

Karpov was still moving quickly, indicating that he was in his prepared analysis, but this retreat seems odd. So often in this variation Black must play ... ♞d5 at some point to blot out White's bishop on d3. Indeed later on Karpov's knight does go to d5.

| 19 | ♛f4 | 33 | ♝g6 | 07 |
|----|------|-----|------|-----|

Karpov had not yet slowed down, but here challenging White's bishop with 19 ... ♝e6 (preparation or not) must be superior. White cannot win with 20 ♖e1 ♞f8 21 d5 cd 22 ♞xd5 ♝xb2 23 ♞c7 on account of 23 ...

117

♛b8! pinning the intrusive knight.

**20 h4!** *50*

The obvious plan is 20 ♖e1 and 21 ♛g4. Perhaps Karpov was ready for that. After Kasparov's more oblique choice Karpov, too, started to think. One of White's threats is the brutal g4-g5, crowding Black's minor pieces off the board and trying to prise open the h-file.

**20 ... ♛d8** *37*

**21 ♞a4** *55*

A fine move. White stops ...♛b6, provokes the weakening ...b5 and threatens to march in with ♞c5 if Black moves his knight from its defensive station at d7.

**21 ... h5** *46*

Forestalling a possible g4.

| 22 | ♖e1 | *65* | b5 | *59* |
|---|---|---|---|---|
| 22 | ♞c3 | *72* | ♛b8 | *60* |
| 24 | ♛e3! | *82* | | |

24 ♞e5 ♞xe5 25 de is obvious but less good, since the white e-pawn is temporarily pinned. The text maintains unpleasant pressure.

| 24 | ... | | b4 | *73* |
|---|---|---|---|---|
| 25 | ♞e4 | *84* | ba | *85* |

If 25 ... ♗xe4 26 ♛xe4 ba 27 ♗c2 g6 28 ♛xc6 or 27 ... ♞f8 28 ba and White retains the initiative.

| 26 | ♞xf6+ | *84* | ♞xf6 | *85* |
|---|---|---|---|---|
| 27 | ba | *84* | ♞d5 | *97* |

At last Black decides to block the diagonal. 27 ... ♞g4 28 ♛c3 is too loosening. As played Karpov stabilises the pawn structure and increases his chances of a draw.

| 28 | ♗xd5 | *86* | cd | *97* |
|---|---|---|---|---|

| 29 | ♞e5 | *88* | ♛d8 | *103* |
|---|---|---|---|---|
| 30 | ♛f3 | *99* | | |

Also tempting is 30 ♞xg6 fg 31 ♛e6+ ♚h7 32 g3 to be followed by ♖e5. Kasparov's choice prevents 30 ... ♛xh4 on account of 31 ♞xg6 fg 32 ♛xd5+. Meanwhile White threatens 31 ♞xg6 and 32 ♖e5.

**30 ... ♖a6** *116*

"Probably the only move" – Khalifman.

| 31 | ♖c1 | *105* | ♚h7 | *127* |
|---|---|---|---|---|
| 32 | ♛h3 | *119* | | |

Preparing to penetrate on c8.

| 32 | ... | | ♖b6 | *135* |
|---|---|---|---|---|
| 33 | ♖c8 | *123* | ♛d6 | *135* |
| 34 | ♛g3 | *126* | | |

Introducing many new tactical threats based on the vis-a-vis of the two queens.

| 34 | ... | | a4 | *137* |
|---|---|---|---|---|
| 35 | ♖a8 | *130* | | |

Winning Black's a-pawn, for if 35 ... ♖b3 36 ♖h8+ ♚xh8 37 ♞xf7+ or 35 ... ♖a6 36 ♞xf7 ♗xf7 37 ♛d3+.

| 35 | ... | | ♛e6 | *143* |
|---|---|---|---|---|
| 36 | ♖xa4 | *133* | ♛f5 | *143* |
| 37 | ♖a7 | *136* | ♖b1+ | *144* |

| 38 | ♔h2 | 136 | ♖c1 | 144 |
| 39 | ♖b7 | 144 | | |

To stop ... ♛b1. In trying to redress the material balance Karpov allows White's attack to flare up again.

| 39 | ... | | ♖c2 | 144 |
| 40 | f3 | 145 | ♖d2 | 147 |
| 41 | ♘d7!! | | | |

The sealed move which Kasparov wrote down and then reinforced, giving onlookers the impression he had changed his mind.

| 41 | ... | | ♖xd4 | 148 |
| 42 | ♘f8+ | 161 | ♔h6 | 150 |

Or 42 ... ♔g8 43 ♖b8.

| 43 | ♖b4!! | 161 | | |

The key move, the point of which is to regain control of f4. Apart from the move played Black has two main choices:

a) 43 ... ♖xb4 44 ab d4 45 b5 d3 46 b6 d2 47 b7 d1♛ 48 b8♛ ♛d2 49 ♘xg6 ♛xg6 50 ♛h8+ ♛h7 51 ♛gxg7 mate – a most unusual variation with four queens on the board.

b) 43 ... ♖d3! puts up the most fight. In his turn White has three choices:

c1) 44 ♖b8 ♗h7 45 ♘e6 fe 46 ♖f8 ♖xa3 47 ♖xf5 ♗xf5 48 ♛g5+ ♔h7 49 ♛xh5+ ♔g8 50 ♛e8+ ♔h7 51 g4 ♖xf3 52 gf ♖xf5 53 ♛xe6 ♖f6 with a draw. If White does not play 51 g4 at once then ... ♖a2 immobilises his kingside pawns and makes the win (if indeed there is one) most problematic.

c2) 44 ♖b8 ♗h7 45 ♖e8 (threat ♖e5) 45 ... ♖d4 (to meet 46 ♖e5 with ♛f4) 46 ♛g5+ ♛xg5 47 hg+ ♔xg5 48 ♘xh7+. This should win now that Black's rook has been lured away from attacking a3.

c3) 44 ♛e1! d4 (to meet 45 ♛c1+ with ♖e3) 45 ♛g3 ♖e3 46 ♖b5 ♛xb5 47 ♛f4+. If 44 ... ♗h7 45 ♖b6+ g6 46 ♛c1+ ♔g7 47 ♘e6+ fe 48 ♖b7+ ♔h8 49 ♛h6 or 48 ... ♔f6 49 ♛h6 winning in both cases. If 44 ... ♛c8 45 ♛e7 ♛f5 46 f4 f6 47 ♘e6 ♖h3+ 48 ♔g1! leaves Black without a decent check.

| 43 | ... | | ♖c4 | 150 |

The line of least resistance.

| 44 | ♖xc4 | 162 | bc | 150 |
| 45 | ♛d6 | 162 | c3 | 150 |
| 46 | ♛d4 | 162 | Resigns | |

If 46 ... ♗h7 47 ♛xc3 with a deadly check coming along the c1-h6 diagonal.

| Kasparov | ½ | ½ | ½ | 1 | 0 | ½ | ½ | 1 | ½ | ½ | ½ | ½ | ½ | 1 | ½ | 1 | 0 | 0 | 0 | ½ | ½ | 1 | 11½ |
| Karpov | ½ | ½ | ½ | 0 | 1 | ½ | ½ | 0 | ½ | ½ | ½ | ½ | ½ | 0 | ½ | 0 | 1 | 1 | 1 | ½ | ½ | 0 | 10½ |

# GAME TWENTY-THREE, 6 October

At 9.34 pm it was all over. Kasparov was still Champion. After playing his 32nd move Karpov realised his chances of pressing home in an ending had evaporated. He waited for Kasparov to return to the board and offered the draw. As Kasparov accepted, the two players shook hands and the crowd rose for a standing ovation. The audience broke into rhythmic clapping. While the players exchanged some words at the table Chief Arbiter Lothar Schmid came over to shake Kasparov's hand and then Karpov's.

The game witnessed an oblique approach by Karpov, who tried to throw the young Champion off balance in a morass of middlegame manoeuvres. But it was Kasparov who struck out with an original rook tour – marching the black queen's rook into the centre of the board, swinging it to the kingside and then suddenly withdrawing the rook to its original square. Grandmasters were baffled by the depth of the conception, but during the period of the rook manoeuvre Karpov's position seemed to make no significant progress. On the 24th move Kasparov sacrificed a pawn and after some anguished thought Karpov finally decided he could not hold the pawn or make any other significant gains.

Karpov must now play a match with Andrei Sokolov to decide Kasparov's next challenger. On the previous day the 23-year-old had defeated Artur Yusupov at Riga with a brilliant comeback to score three victories in the last four games. If Karpov wins against Sokolov in their match set for Linares in Jan/Feb 1987 we face a Kasparov-Karpov IV contest next year.

**Karpov-Kasparov**
*Hedgehog*

**1   ♘f3   00**

The first time in this match that 1 d4 or 1 e4 has not been played. This indicates that Karpov could find nothing against the Queen's Indian and that he was still not prepared to face the Scheveningen Sicilian.

| 1 | ... | | ♘f6 | 02 |
|---|---|---|---|---|
| 2 | c4 | 00 | b6 | 02 |
| 3 | g3 | 01 | c5 | 03 |
| 4 | ♗g2 | 01 | ♗b7 | 03 |
| 5 | 0-0 | 02 | g6 | 04 |
| 6 | d4 | 05 | cd | 04 |
| 7 | ♕xd4 | 06 | ♗g7 | 05 |

**8** ♘c3  *07*  **d6**  *08*

Establishing a super-solid hedgehog, spines abristle. After 8 ... ♘c6 9 ♕f4 ♖c8 10 ♖d1 d6 11 b3 ♘e4 12 ♘xe4 ♗xa1 13 ♗a3 ♗g7 14 ♘fg5 Black is in trouble, Ribli-Kouatly, Lucerne (World Team Championship) 1985.

**9**  ♖d1  *14*  ♘bd7  *09*
**10**  **b3**  *22*  ♖c8  *19*

Further caution. 10 ... 0-0 permits 11 ♕h4 followed by ♗h6.

**11**  ♗b2  *23*  **0-0**  *32*
**12**  ♕e3  *46*  ♖e8  *36*
**13**  ♖ac1  *52*  **a6**  *41*
**14**  ♗a1  *59*  ♖c5  *42*
**15**  **a4**  *69*  ♕a8  *47*
**16**  ♘e1  *73*  ♖f5  *65*

A remarkable move. It looks extraordinarily naive to attack White's kingside in this fashion, but Black's position is sufficiently flexible to stand this adventure.

This withdrawal of the rook proves how little White can achieve once a hedgehog has been set up and is fully functional.

**20**  ♗b2  *93*  ♖cc8  *103*
**21**  ♗a3  *98*  ♘c5  *104*
**22**  ♖b1  *99*  ♘e6  *107*
**23**  ♕d3  *123*  ♘c7  *112*
**24**  ♘f4  *127*  **b5**  *115*
**25**  **cb**  *128*  **ab**  *118*
**26**  ♘xb5  *128*

Black has absolutely freed himself with ... b5. Not 26 ab? ♕a7+.

**26**  **...**  ♘xb5  *119*
**27**  ♕xb5  *128*  ♕xb5  *121*
**28**  **ab**  *128*  ♖b8  *121*
**29**  ♗b2  *129*  ♖b7  *127*

Much the best. 29 ... ♖xb5 30 ♗xf6 ♗xf6 31 ♘d5 gives White small chances.

**30**  **b6**  *135*  ♖eb8  *130*
**31**  **b4**  *137*  ♘d7  *132*
**32**  ♗xg7  *140*

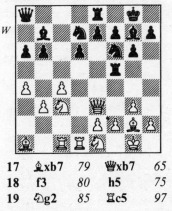

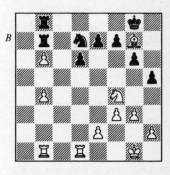

**17**  ♗xb7  *79*  ♕xb7  *65*
**18**  **f3**  *80*  **h5**  *75*
**19**  ♘g2  *85*  ♖c5  *97*

Karpov offered a **draw**, leaving Kasparov in retention of his title.

| Kasparov | ½ | ½ | ½ | 1 | 0 | ½ | ½ | 1 | ½ | ½ | ½ | ½ | ½ | 1 | ½ | 1 | 0 | 0 | 0 | ½ | ½ | 1 | ½ | **12** |
| Karpov | ½ | ½ | ½ | 0 | 1 | ½ | ½ | 0 | ½ | ½ | ½ | ½ | ½ | 0 | ½ | 0 | 1 | 1 | 1 | ½ | ½ | 0 | ½ | **11** |

# GAME TWENTY-FOUR, 8 October

There was a feeling of anticlimax about today's game, which was comfortably held by the former World Champion who defended precisely against Kasparov's aggressive play to reach an easily drawn rook ending. The feeling among the assembled cognoscenti was that peace was imminent, but to everyone's amazement Karpov sealed a move. However, the draw was agreed the next day without resumption.

Karpov looked slightly tired today, but considering the disappointment he must feel at failing to regain his title he still played toughly and accurately.

**Kasparov-Karpov**
*Queen's Indian Defence*

| | | | | | |
|---|---|---|---|---|---|
| 1 | d4 | 00 | ♘f6 | 00 |
| 2 | c4 | 00 | e6 | 00 |
| 3 | ♘f3 | 00 | b6 | 00 |
| 4 | g3 | 01 | ♗b7 | 01 |
| 5 | ♗g2 | 01 | ♗b4+ | 01 |
| 6 | ♗d2 | 02 | a5 | 01 |
| 7 | 0-0 | 04 | 0-0 | 01 |
| 8 | ♗g5 | 11 | ♗e7 | 01 |

8 ♗f4 intending c5 followed by a3 was an interesting alternative.

| | | | | | |
|---|---|---|---|---|---|
| 9 | ♕c2 | 12 | h6 | 05 |
| 10 | ♗xf6 | 16 | ♗xf6 | 05 |
| 11 | ♘c3 | 17 | g6 | 26 |
| 12 | ♖ad1 | 35 | d6 | 30 |
| 13 | h4 | 38 | h5 | 42 |
| 14 | e4 | 47 | ♘d7 | 48 |
| 15 | e5 | 61 | ♗g7 | 50 |

| | | | | |
|---|---|---|---|---|
| 16 | d5 | 75 | | |

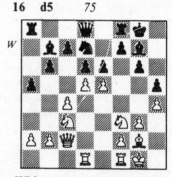

White seems to have a dangerous initiative and this aggressive thrust is in accordance with Kasparov's style, but Karpov shows that his position is resilient enough.

Instead Botvinnik suggests 16 ed cd 17 ♘g5 and White is better.

| | | | | |
|---|---|---|---|---|
| 16 | ... | | ♘xe5 | 56 |
| 17 | ♘xe5 | 75 | ♗xe5 | 56 |

122

| 18 | de | 76 | ♗xg2 | 56 |
|----|----|----|------|-----|
| 19 | ef+ | 76 | ♔xf7 | 65 |
| 20 | ♔xg2 | 77 | ♗xc3 | 66 |
| 21 | ♕xc3 | 79 | ♕f6 | 68 |
| 22 | ♕xf6+ | 91 | ♔xf6 | 68 |
| 23 | a4 | 94 | ♖ae8 | 72 |
| 24 | ♖fe1 | 95 | ♖xe1 | 82 |
| 25 | ♖xe1 | 96 | ♖d8 | 82 |
| 26 | ♖d1 | 102 | c6 | 91 |
| 27 | ♔f3 | 106 | ♔e5 | 109 |
| 28 | ♔e3 | 112 | ♖f8 | 125 |
| 29 | f3 | 126 | ♖h8 | 130 |

Kasparov's initiative has evaporated in the face of Karpov's active defence.

| 30 | ♖e1 | 130 | ♖b8 | 130 |
|----|----|----|------|-----|
| 31 | ♔d3+ | 131 | ♔f6 | 130 |

The game has become something of a non-event and meanders peacefully towards its inevitable conclusion.

| 32 | ♖e4 | 135 | d5 | 134 |
|----|----|----|----|-----|
| 33 | cd | 139 | cd | 134 |
| 34 | ♖e2 | 142 | b5 | 135 |
| 35 | ♔d4 | 142 | ba | 137 |
| 36 | ♔xd5 | 142 | ♖b3 | 138 |
| 37 | ♔e4 | 143 | ♖b4+ | 139 |
| 38 | ♔d5 | 143 | ♖b5+ | 143 |
| 39 | ♔d4 | 145 | ♖b4+ | 146 |
| 40 | ♔d5 | 145 | ♖b3 | 146 |
| 41 | ♔e4 | 146 | ♖b4+ | 156 |

This move was sealed by Karpov but the game was agreed drawn without resumption.

Kasparov ½ ½ ½ 1 0 ½ ½ 1 ½ ½ ½ ½ ½ 1 ½ 1 0 0 0 ½ ½ 1 ½ ½  12½

Karpov  ½ ½ ½ 0 1 ½ ½ 0 ½ ½ ½ ½ ½ 0 ½ 0 1 1 1 ½ ½ 0 ½ ½  11½

Over the past two years Kasparov and Karpov have contested three bitter matches involving 96 games. Kasparov has now edged into a lifetime lead by 13 games to 12 with 71 draws. In this last match Kasparov's quality of play has been clearly superior. In terms of ideas Kasparov has dominated, but Karpov kept himself afloat with tremendous pre-game preparation combined with an iron display of will power when three games in arrears. If Kasparov can maintain his brilliance while eradicating his unforced errors he stands an excellent chance of overshadowing the mercurial American genius Bobby Fischer. London was lucky indeed to have hosted the first ever part of a world championship match involving Soviet grandmasters playing outside the Soviet Union, and this will have contributed immeasurably to the popularity of chess in the UK.

# INTERVIEW WITH KASPAROV

After the 24th game was adjourned co-author Ray Keene visited Kasparov at his Leningrad hide-out on Stone Island. Over a sumptuous dinner of caviar, stuffed pike and stuffed turkey, several questions prepared by co-author David Goodman were put to the World Champion.

Before we started Kasparov expressed his annoyance that game 24 was still in progress. He asked " Would you play on against anyone in this position?" and added that members of the audience had cried "Shame" when the game was adjourned. His answers to the major questions were as follows:

*Q: What was the best game of the match?*
A: No doubt, game 16. It was an extremely complex game. Karpov was never better and after I played ♗xd3 I had everything worked out.

*Q: Did you believe you would recover from your collapse?*
A: Yes, after game 19 one of my assistants Viktor Litvinov spelt it out to me that I only had to make 12 points to win. Once I understood that the rest was easy.

*Q: Who is favourite in the Karpov-Sokolov match?*
A: Karpov for sure. Next year I know I will play Karpov again.

*Q: What changes would you like to make in FIDE?*
A: Campomanes must go. It is war to the death with him as far as I am concerned. I will do everything I can to remove him.

*Q: What are your plans now?*
A: I intend to play in various tournaments: maybe a short match against Nigel Short and I also plan to be a judge at the Miss World contest in London in November. I want to go on a world tour to promote chess and set up a franchise for the Botvinnik school.